D1503174

Senior Savvy

Copyright © 1993
by Kenneth A. Stern

All rights reserved

No part of this book may be used or reproduced in any manner
whatsoever without written permission except in the case of brief
quotations embodied in critical articles or reviews.

Library of Congress Catalog Card Number: 93-85482
ISBN: 0-9637698-0-4

For information contact:

Segue Capital, Inc.
17065 Via del Campo, #101
San Diego, CA 92127
Tel: (619) 485-0404

Cover Design: The Art Ranch

Typesetting: Sandy Reeve/STAX

Editorial Consultant: Write Now! (619) 449-4044

Printing: Vanard Lithographers

Printed in the United States of America

SENIOR SAVVY

Simple Strategies and Advanced Techniques
to Control, Preserve and Maximize Your Estate

by
KENNETH A. STERN

Technical contributions by
ROBERT SMYKOWSKI, ESQ.
and
BURGESS HALLUMS

This book could never have been completed without the hard work of a remarkable team of professionals. Paul Hoffer's determination and marketing skills and Robert Smykowski's unlimited wealth of knowledge in estate law. Burgess Hallums and the whole Segue Capital staff deserve thanks for keeping our practice running during my sabbatical. My thanks also to Centurion Counsel and Jack Heilbron for their knowledge of, and assistance in, securities. Finally, my deepest gratitude to my incredibly supportive family, Norton, Sherrie and Scott Stern.

Kenneth A. Stern

INTRODUCTION

Your retirement years should be the best years of your life. However, upon retirement, most seniors have many more pitfalls to overcome than working individuals. The primary reason is that everything you have worked for and accumulated has to last ... there are no more second chances. You need to survive the economic uncertainties brought about by political changes and economic cycles. And you will go experience many changes taking place regarding medical care: how benefits will be provided and how governmental changes will affect Medicare and Medicaid. Through all of this you need to stay happy and healthy. A long illness can deplete your life savings. Therefore, it is critical to know how to protect your assets.

You need to make sure your money lasts through constant market fluctuations, interest rate swings, tax law changes and soaring inflation. It is a fact that inflation affects the retiree more than any other segment of the population. Just look at the ever-increasing costs of travel, leisure and health care.

It is critical that your money be safe from investment scandals, banking, insurance failures and other problems with "guaranteed" investments.

Finally, provided you overcome these obstacles, you need to stay well informed in order to avoid unnecessary costs and fees associated with probate, death taxes and capital gains. You also need to prepare for the emotional effects, delays and the responsibility of managing your estate and finances without a spouse.

If all of the above sounds gloomy, it shouldn't. People fail financially for two reasons: procrastination and lack of knowledge. In fact, I think that people procrastinate because of lack of knowledge.

This book will give you the knowledge; it's up to you to *control, preserve and maximize* your assets. If you can accomplish these three tasks, you will experience *the happiest years of your life during your retirement.*

PART ONE
THE FINANCIAL PLAN

PART TWO
ESTATE PLANNING

PART THREE
HEALTH CARE PLANNING

CHAPTER 14

CHAPTER 15

PART FOUR
WHERE TO INVEST YOUR MONEY

CHAPTER 16

CHAPTER 17

CONCLUSION

APPENDIX

PART ONE

THE FINANCIAL PLAN

CHAPTER 1

How To Create a Plan

If you planned to drive across the country, you would never start without a map and an idea of where you were going. In the same way, you cannot successfully manage your funds without a plan. If you try, you will spend too much time, waste money, and you will endure needless aggravation from mistakes that could have been avoided. These mistakes include such problems as excessive fees paid to professionals, bad advice, and inflated expenses related to an unexpected death or illness.

The mature American must prepare now for an extended life span, unexpected hyper-inflation, higher taxes and economic uncertainty. The sad truth is that public and private retirement programs will not pay the majority of your bills, leaving the burden on your shoulders. In fact, the average retiree will spend 80% of his or her annual pre-retirement income to maintain his or her retirement lifestyle. Planning for retirement would be simple if you were assured that the cost of retirement would be just 80% of your pre-retirement income. Instead, inflation is an serious factor to consider. The following chart shows how $40,000 has shrunk to barely $10,000 over the past 20 years because of inflation.

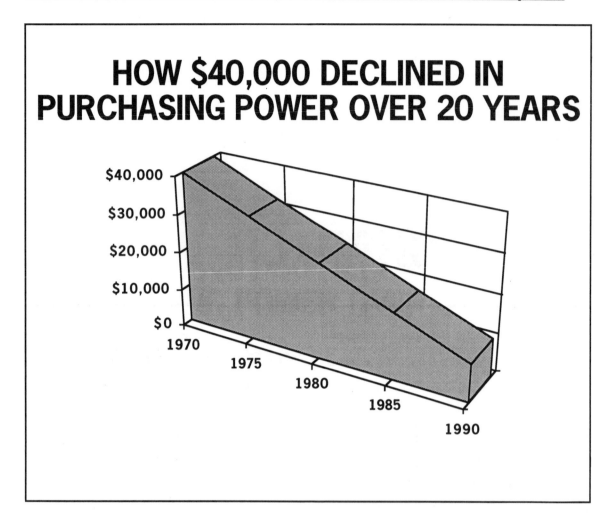

HOW $40,000 DECLINED IN PURCHASING POWER OVER 20 YEARS

Most people do not plan for retirement. Why? The main reason is because they are misinformed about the true extent of the retirement gap. A common myth is that Social Security and pensions will take care of the retiree. Unfortunately Social Security and pensions usually do not account for even half of the required retirement income. This leaves the average retiree with the burden of coming up with the other half of his or her living expenses from personal savings. Furthermore, in the current economic environment, we are even experiencing cuts in retirement benefits and reduced medical coverage. Either one of these could unexpectedly result in increased expenses for every retiree.

I am baffled when I hear that someone retires and invests money not knowing what he or she needs or what he or she wants to accomplish. Chances are, that retiree will either take too much (or too little) risk, invest too much (or too little), or invest in areas that do not accurately reflect a retiree's needs and desires.

STEP ONE -- CREATE YOUR PLAN

First and foremost, it is imperative that you make a list of your goals and challenges. If you do not know what you are trying to accomplish, you cannot make a plan. Start by making a list of short-term and long-term (six month, three years, and ten years) financial goals and personal goals.

YOUR LIST OF GOALS MAY LOOK LIKE THIS:

1. I will not outlive my money and I will make sure my family is well provided for.

2. I will gift money to my grandchildren.

3. I will not lose control of my estate because of probate or medical costs. I will make certain that if my spouse and I ever need to use our life savings for a medical crisis, my spouse will be well provided for.

4. I will pay less in both income and estate taxes.

5. I will make certain that my money is protected if I have to enter a nursing home. I know I cannot afford to pay the cost out of pocket because the result will leave my family without money.

6. I will visit Europe.

7. I will shoot an 80 for eighteen holes of golf.

8. I will notify my family that in the event of a terminal illness that I do not want to be kept alive on life support systems.

Be sure your list of goals has a mix of both business, personal and recreational items. If you do not have a goal to strive for when you wake up in the morning, you have no challenge. Without a challenge, as minor as it may seem, you lose the precious life force.

In my daily travels, I have seen that the happiest retirees wake up in the morning, list out their goals for the day, and then set out to accomplish them. And make sure you have a hobby or an interest when you retire. Undoubtedly, your retirement will be that much more enriching.

Now that your goals are in place, work backwards. *Never do any investing until you know what it is that you are trying to accomplish!*

Suppose I asked you, "What rate of return do you need on your money so, regardless of any situation, you are sure you will never outlive your money?" Most people do not know the answer.

If I asked you, "Where are you invested *and what are your investment goals?*" You and others would not have an answer to this question.

THEREFORE, MY NEXT QUESTIONS ARE:

- How did you decide to invest where you did if you didn't know the return you need?

- Are you taking too much risk?

- What is the most your portfolio could lose?

- Is your return high enough?

- How will inflation impact it?

- Are your assets protected from probate?

Although each person's plan is different and tries to accomplish different goals, the questions are usually fairly similar. First ask the questions you want your plan to answer, then begin the creation of your plan.

THE QUESTIONS YOU SHOULD BE ASKING YOURSELF MIGHT INCLUDE:

1. If I live another forty years, will the money I currently have run out? What interest rate, or dividend do I need, to be certain my money will not run out? How will inflation impact these figures?

2. In any given year, how much could my portfolio lose? And, just as important, how much can my portfolio stand to lose and still accomplish my goals?

3. Is my portfolio being maximized? Is it possible to pay less in taxes to keep more of my money? Or, can I get the same return in a less risky investment?

4. If one spouse passes on, can the other spouse manage the portfolio? Will there be any delays or costs because of a death?

STEP TWO -- SOURCES OF RETIREMENT INCOME

To understand your portfolio better, it is essential to know all the sources of your income. A good exercise for you to do is to compute your total monthly or yearly income. Once you know your total, change it to percentages. Know how much comes from Social Security, your retirement plan through work and your investments.

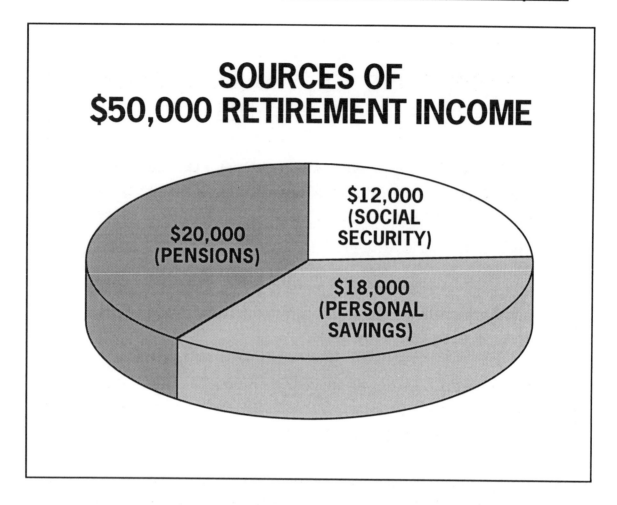

SOURCES OF
$50,000 RETIREMENT INCOME

$12,000
(SOCIAL
SECURITY)

$20,000
(PENSIONS)

$18,000
(PERSONAL
SAVINGS)

After completing this exercise you will know all the sources of your income, how much of your savings is needed for income, and the interest rate required. *Once you know the percentage you need to have saved from your funds, increase your savings percentage by at least 10%.*

There is a reason for the 10% buffer. You never know if Social Security will be reduced, if your employer will cut retirement benefits, or if inflation will increase beyond your projections.

> **When speaking of Social Security, it is important to note that, historically, taxes on Social Security benefits rise faster than income taxes. Newly proposed legislation may tax benefits even more, lowering your true Social Security benefit. Don`t rely on Social Security!**

If you are living to close to your current needs, you can get into financial trouble that would otherwise have been avoided.

STEP THREE -- FINDING YOUR REQUIRED RETURN

Now that the first two steps of building a financial plan are complete, the third step is to find your *Required Rate of Return.*

Always allow for the worst scenario. Let's start with this rule of thumb: Retirement will cost 80% of your pre-retirement income, increasing each year with the cost of living. Assume that inflation will average much higher than you expect (at least 5%) and assume also that you will be retired for at least 40 years (you might retire at 60 and live to be 100 years old). Although this may sound far-fetched, current studies show that living until 100 years of age has become increasingly common. In fact, the fastest growing age group in America is the over-85 age group. Next, discount the value of Social Security as a source for secure retirement income. Although these parameters may sound unreasonable, many people who retired fifteen years ago thought they would only be living for fifteen more years.

This is what I call *Bullet Proofing* your portfolio. If you can still retire comfortably after satisfying the above requirements, chances are you will be successful in retirement. Once bullet-proofed, you don't have to worry about investments, interest rate swings, recessions, or living past your expected life span. You are covered! Now, when your head hits the pillow at night, all you should be thinking about is tomorrow, your hobby or your grandchildren, not finances!

Now that you know the necessary parameters, you are now on your way to finding your required rate of return. Your required rate of return is defined as the percentage of return you need to receive on your investment portfolio in order to avoid outliving your money. Based on the above scenario, if you know all you need to earn is 8% to accomplish all your goals, should you take any unnecessary risks? Should you invest in aggressive mutual funds, stocks, commodities, or anything risky where you could lose substantial amounts of money? If you can reduce your risk by avoiding these investments, you will not have to allow for losses from bad investments. This will increase, or secure, your return with less risk.

EXAMPLES OF BULLET PROOFING

FIRST SCENARIO

Let's assume you were making $80,000 per year, prior to your retirement, and you will be retiring at age 65. You will need at least $64,000 per year income starting in the first year, rising at 5% per year for inflation. In ten years you will need $79,000; in 20 years you will need about $100,000, and so on. Assume further that you will receive $30,000 per year from your employee retirement benefit plan and $11,000 in Social Security.

Basically, this means you will need to generate $23,000 per year out of your pocket, rising at 5% per year to live. Now, divide $23,000 by 8% (using the assumption that 8% is your required return), and it will tell you the dollar amount you need to generate $23,000 per year without touching principal. In this case, that number is $290,000. If you assume that after the first year you will need 5% more in income to maintain your standard of living to keep up with inflation, you will now need to begin using principal. The bottom line is that your principal will be spent in about forty years if interest on your money or the value of your money doesn't rise. (See Compounding Table in Appendix.)

Obviously, the above scenario is very close to bullet proof. However, that scenario counts on Social Security, no extra medical expenses, and leaves little room for error. You can calculate the same numbers using 9% or 10% as your required return. You would need less to invest but if you use higher, perhaps unreasonable percentages, you need to consider the riskier investment options which should never be something you count on for retirement. Not many people earn 10% on their entire portfolio, on average. As I said earlier, you should always use at least a 10% cushion when formulating your plans. Figure all the numbers and then add 10%.

SECOND SCENARIO

Take a different look by assuming instead that you have $300,000 in savings, and only need $23,000 every year for income. Your numbers will be different. At an 8% interest rate, the income on $300,000 is higher – in fact, it is $24,000 per year. If the extra $1,000 of income is reinvested until needed in an effort to keep up with inflation, your money should not run out for over 50 years. *The power of Compounding*

10

Interest is unbelievable. When investing, any amount, no matter how small, could make a major difference in your retirement lifestyle.

To be completely bullet proof, have an extra 10% over the original $290,000. Or, to be absolutely sure, do the same calculations but on 90% of your assets, holding back 10%. With this 10% you have spending money to occasionally spoil yourself – exceed your budget, tour the world, help your children, gamble, or try to earn more money in certain investments with a higher degree of risk. Of course, you could also keep this money absolutely safe and use it as your safety net. Regardless of what you do with the extra 10%, you know that if you lose every penny of this 10% it will not affect your lifestyle.

Why not find a hobby that you enjoy and which might earn money? Many retirees purchase rental property in order to keep busy, and then make a great deal of profit at it by becoming an expert in the "business" of their hobby.

Although the financial planning exercises above may sound obvious, if they are not performed to some degree you will be investing blindly.

BY KNOWING THE ANSWERS TO THE ABOVE QUESTIONS, YOU SHOULD HAVE NO DOUBT AS TO:

1. What return you need to retire.
2. How much money you need to have saved.
3. What your yearly budget should be.
4. How much you can afford to lose.

With careful, proper planning, higher inflation or lower interest rates should not greatly affect your golden years.

Now that you have figured your personal needs and understand what is required, the next step is to review the asset allocation and investment chapters to see how to invest. The Estate Planning chapters discuss how to hold title to your assets, protect those assets, and distribute your assets. To understand how to implement your financial plan and reduce taxes, refer to the Table of Contents under the Investment Sections.

SIMPLE FORMULAS

Obviously you can look at all the calculations and become exasperated. It can be difficult, by why make it so? All you need to know are a few simple techniques for basic planning purposes.

DETERMINING YOUR NET WORTH

Do you think you know your net worth? If I were the probate judge, would I know? What would it say on your final tax return? The point is there are many different ways to compute net worth. Some net worth statements will have to be used to make your plan while others are used for specific purposes such as probate.

One of the reasons why it is important to figure net worth is to plan for estate taxes. After an estate reaches $600,000 in assets the tax levied on the estate is very high.

For many people, talking of estates valued at more than $600,000 sounds extremely high. But is it really?

Assume a couple retires and their estate is worth $300,000. Assume the two spouses are 65 years of age and have been very conservative with their investments. After taking the income they need, the estate is earning only 5% per year. Let's assume that 20 years later both spouses die. Three hundred thousand dollars' growth at 5% per annum for 20 years will produce an estate valued at $800,000. But, wait! Add up all the life insurance polices – the wife had $50,000 and the husband had $100,000. The estate that originally was $300,000, growing at only 5% increased to over $950,000! Let me thank you in advance on behalf of Uncle Sam for the high estate taxes you will pay.

The problem is this – every person or married couple is entitled to a one-time estate tax exclusion which means your estate will be free of estate taxes up to $600,000. After that, the estate taxes are among the highest and most expensive taxes currently in existence. The tax rate ranges from 37% to a high of 55%.

Let's say a person's estate is worth $2,000,000 upon death. If you subtract the allowed $600,000, the estate burden is $1,400,000. The tax burden on $1,400,000 is over $600,000!

This is not a negotiable sum or a figure you can ignore. If you owe estate taxes they must be paid within nine months after the death. Using the previous example, how many of our beneficiaries can write a check for $600,000? Real estate, stocks or cash will have to be sold to pay this tax burden. And if you wanted the real estate to stay in the family – too bad. If your beneficiaries cannot come up with the money to pay the tax, the IRS will be delighted to liquidate the assets. But there are some solutions to the estate tax problem.

The current administration has been working toward lowering the estate tax exclusion to $200,000 per person. If this change becomes imminent, you might even consider at that time gifting as much as necessary up to the $1,200,000 that married couples are currently allowed to gift. This would ensure that you would be able to take advantage of the full $1,200,000.

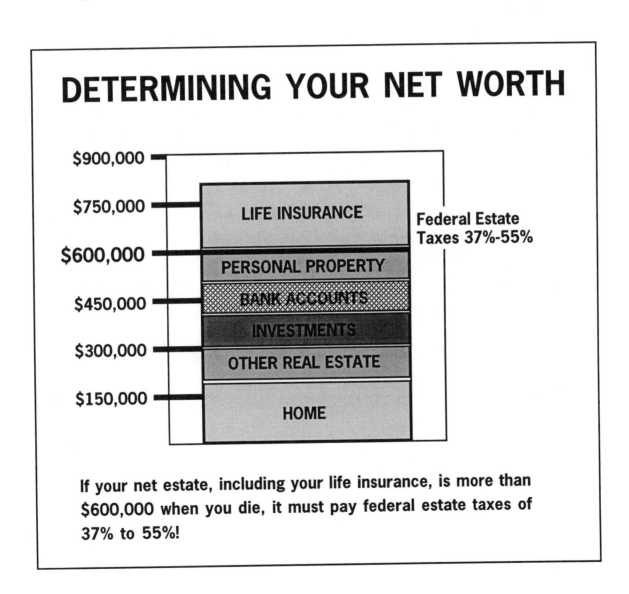

DETERMINING YOUR NET WORTH

If your net estate, including your life insurance, is more than $600,000 when you die, it must pay federal estate taxes of 37% to 55%!

COMPOUNDING INTEREST

First, I refer to compounding interest throughout this book because *compound interest must be the eighth wonder of the world.* In the Appendix you can see how the present value of a dollar compounds at different interest rates.

Furthermore, if you continually add to your investment, the return on your money will appear almost overwhelming. That is why so much time is spent discussing dollar-cost averaging of systematic savings.

THE RULE OF 72

One very effective, yet easy, formula, is that of *The Rule of 72.*

For planning purposes you may want to know when your money will double. Perhaps you have a goal. Therefore, finding out at what point your money will double is not only important but easy to determine. Divide 72 by the interest rate. Assume you expect to earn 10%. So, 72 divided by 10% equals 7.2 years. Then look at the difference in the length of time it takes you to double your money by using different interest rates. For instance, 72 divided by 3% equals 23.6 years. And 72 divided by 5.5% is 13 years.

THE RULE OF 72
To find out the length of time required to double your money, divide 72 by the interest rate:

72 ÷ 10% = 7.2 YEARS

CHAPTER 2

Inflation: A Real Threat

Inflation is very much like the movie "Jaws." Just when you thought it was safe to go back in the water, *watch out!* The same holds true for inflation. Just when you forget to count on inflation, *watch out!*

Inflation is even more critical for the retired American because usually the retiree's income is fixed. Even if your income does rise, it often does so at rates far below the inflation rate.

Back when you were growing up, or perhaps raising a family, inflation was not such a critical issue. From 1969 through 1979, there was a 50% loss in purchasing power. Although that sounds drastic, it was nothing compared to the 20% loss of purchasing power in the two years from the beginning of 1980 until the end of 1981 due to inflation. *Today, it takes one dollar to buy what 29 cents bought in 1970, and what 12 cents bought in 1945.*

Inflation is extremely hard to regulate. In other words, inflation is too much money competing to buy the level of goods and services available in the marketplace. I am under the impression that if you rely on the inflation figures provided by the media, you will find that those figures are inaccurate when applied to the lifestyle of the typical retiree. To arrive at the inflation numbers you read about, a "typical market basket of goods" is used. But is the typical retiree's "basket of goods" the same as that of a working family?

The mature American spends money on household goods such as tissue paper and toothpaste, travel and recreation. Compare the costs of these items over the last five years, and I'll bet it is higher than you expected. Compare travel costs or hobby and leisure time costs – golf in particular.

Of course, one of the most critical expenses is health care. No one can tell the retiree that health care costs are only increasing 5% annually. I have a difficult time believing that the retirees' inflation rate is averaging under 5%.

Approximately twenty years ago, if you retired with $40,000 to invest, that amount would have had to increase to almost $120,000 just to keep pace with inflation. Today the average retiree has an expected life span of over 22 years. Many people believe that in ten years the average life span will be over 30 years. But even using the average of 22 years, it is very difficult just to keep up the pace of inflation.

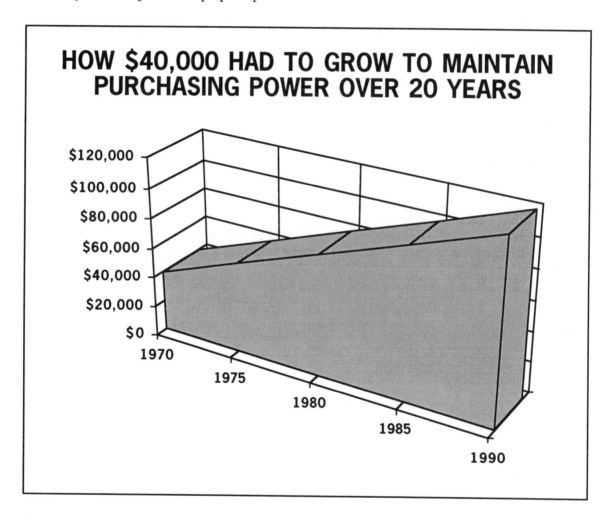

Consider the following chart, "Effects of Inflation and Taxes on Investment Returns." Note that if your investments earned 8% over the last 20 years, your true annualized return after inflation and taxes was only 1.15%. In today's economy, we are seeing safe investments earning as little as 3% to 4%. Although economic experts insist inflation is low, do you really believe the average mature American's inflation rate is under 4%? I doubt it!

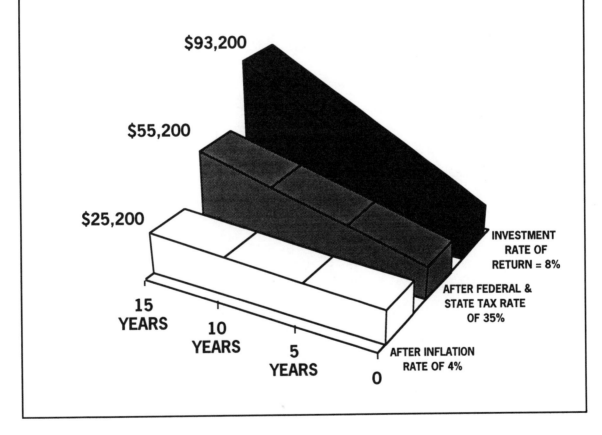

EFFECTS OF INFLATION AND TAXES ON INVESTMENT RETURNS

ANNUALIZED REAL RETURN OVER 20 YEARS AFTER INFLATION AND TAXES = 1.15%

(8% GROSS RETURN, MINUS FEDERAL AND STATE TAXES, MINUS INFLATION)

ASSUMING YOU ARE STARTING WITH $20,000

The bottom line is that inflation is real and is a valid problem. Even if you are currently retiring in a low inflationary environment, don't lower your guard. If you do not respect the real possibility of hyper-inflation, you may ruin your retirement plan. You must prepare for the unexpected. You've lived through it. Don't forget what your parents *never* expected -- their own loss of financial dignity.

They did not plan to fail; they failed to plan!

CHAPTER 3

Employment Retirement Benefits:
How To Maximize Them

Usually, upon retirement from employment, you will need to make a decision regarding retirement benefits: take a lump sum distribution or take the income in regular installments, usually paid on a monthly basis. The income choices might include guaranteed income for your lifetime, you and your spouse's lifetime, or possibly for a specific, guaranteed number of years. If: (1) you want nothing to do with managing money; (2) the monthly income your company offers is, in your opinion, more than sufficient for the rest of your life; (3) you will never need an emergency lump sum distribution; and, (4) you believe the company from which you are retiring will be around longer than you, then you may want to choose to select the income option. You will never have to worry about your money – the check will come regularly, and you will simply enjoy your retirement – provided all is well with your company and the pension policy is for the length of your retirement. Even so, be sure to read the Medicaid chapter before making this decision.

Every case varies, but usually electing the income option has major drawbacks when viewed from the perspective of maximizing your money.

ACCESS TO PRINCIPAL

Technically, when taking an income option you annuitize your money, resulting not only in your loss of access to the principal, but the ability to change anything regarding your selection once your decision has been made.

Even if the monthly income sounds wonderful, question it. Everyone is in business to make money, so your pension company is not going to give you an income so high that they will not earn money too. *If it sounds too good to be true, work the numbers – numbers don't lie!*

Assume that you retire at age 60 and have a choice of taking a lump sum deposit of $100,000 or monthly income in the amount of $835. Assume that your income would be guaranteed for both you and your spouse's lifetime up to thirty years. Basically, by forfeiting the $100,000 you would receive a total over the thirty years of $300,000 of income. Doesn't that sound great? But look back. Do you realize that that does not even equal an annual return of 4% return? Your annualized return is *under 4%, and you never get your $100,000 back!*

Instead, assume you take your lump sum retirement of $100,000 and roll the funds into a *IRA (Individual Retirement Account)*. Inside the IRA you invest in a *United States Government Bond* earning 8%. You will receive $660 per month and get your

$100,000 back at the end of thirty years, guaranteed by the United States government, arguably one of the safest investment vehicles in the world! Although it looks attractive to take the extra $175 in monthly income offered by your pension plan, it would cost you. See how you are lured by the supposedly higher interest?

IS YOUR COMPANY GOING TO LIVE LONGER THAN YOU?

If your company is responsible for providing your monthly income, are you sure the pension is properly funded and insured? Are you willing to take the chance? What if the obligation of paying your income is that of an insurance company? How strong and solvent is that company?

Almost all major pension plans are regulated and guaranteed through the *Pension Benefit Guaranty Corporation (PBGC).* This is the insurance company to the pensions much like the FDIC is to the bank. It has been said that the PBGC is currently operating at a $2.5 billion deficit! By 1998, this deficit could reach at much as $18 billion!

These numbers are real and scary. Many of the large corporations' pensions are underfunded. This means they are probably using the employees working today to pay off the retirees, but there is a current short-fall. As workers continue to retire, a problem will surely arise. Currently almost $40 billion in benefits by corporate pension plans are underfunded!

Another concern if you do decide to take the income is whether to: (1) take the option on the highest income but for only the former worker's lifetime (after his/her death income stops); (2) take joint lifetime income, income payable to you and your spouse; or, (3) take income for a guaranteed number of years, even if a death occurs.

This is a tough question and the answer is different for every plan. If, for example, option one pays you $100 more per month than option two, try this: take option one but reinvest the extra $100 per month. If you retire at 65 years of age and think you will live until 80, that's $100 per month for fifteen years. Based on an 8% interest rate, that will grow to over $34,000. Assuming the retirement stops at age 80 as a result of a death, the $34,000 will generate over $200 per month without touching principal. Keep on trying this scenario over again, making the age of death closer and closer each time, until you can see the "break even" point.

Another popular tactic is to take the extra money from option one and buy a life insurance policy. Check to see how much insurance you can buy for the extra income under option one. You might be surprised how much insurance that money would buy!

Of course, be certain you can qualify for insurance before choosing this option. Also, be sure at this age the insurance rate is permanent and will not rise annually.

CHAPTER 4

Social Security:
How Secure Is It?

The Social Security system was created by an act of Congress in 1935 and Social Security benefits now account for 20% to 30% of the average retiree's income. Although many people only think of Social Security as old age benefits, it really is much more complex. The principal topic for this discussion is the *Old Age and Survivors Insurance Program* which provides monthly benefits to retirees, widows, dependents, spouses and divorced spouses (contingent upon their eligibility). *Medicare,* which is also a function of Social Security for which you will become eligible when you reach the age of 65, will be covered in an upcoming chapter.

Before going any further, however, let me warn you to be careful of relying too heavily on Social Security benefits. You may have heard talk that Social Security benefits may be cut, taxed at a higher percentage rate, or changed dramatically.

These rumors of change are not without some truth. As a result of our longer life span, the average retiree will receive more in Social Security benefits than the system was originally designed to distribute. Many people consider Social Security similar to a Ponzi

Scheme, a fraudulent investment practice that promises high returns. What happens, in fact, is that existing investors in a Ponzi Scheme are paid extremely high amounts of money, which is taken from the principal of new investors who are, in turn, paid off by the next level of new investors. Sooner or later, almost every Ponzi Scheme collapses under its own weight. That is what many people feel will eventually happen to Social Security, because those working now are paying for retirees. When all the Baby Boomers retire, the coffers will be depleted.

HOW TO OBTAIN BENEFITS AND RECEIVE INFORMATION

If you are wondering if you are eligible for benefits, or what those benefits will be at different ages, call the local Social Security office in your area. *The Social Security Administration's new national, toll-free phone number is*

1-800-772-1213.

Benefits are not paid until you file. It is important to file *at least three months prior* to the time you are eligible to receive benefits. This is true for both income benefits and Medicare. Also, remember that the Social Security Administration is not always correct. If you feel there is an error in computing your benefits, it is your right to dispute the decision and have your case reviewed. Frequently, Social Security does makes errors and finds in your favor. It will cost you nothing to have your case reviewed and you do not need to engage the services of an attorney. Many senior centers have attorneys on staff who will meet with you free of charge. Call your local "Area for the Aging" to find out about the availability of this service.

WHEN TO TAKE SOCIAL SECURITY BENEFITS

A person eligible for Social Security benefits must choose between taking full benefits, at 65 years of age or a taking a reduced amount beginning at age 62. My philosophy is that it usually makes sense to take benefits early, especially if you don't need the money for a few years.

REMEMBER ALWAYS TO DO YOUR MATH -- NUMBERS DON'T LIE

Most mature Americans think it is better to wait until they are 65 to begin receiving their Social Security benefits. If you don't need the money right away and will get more money by waiting until age 65, why not?

Here's why: If you were, instead, to receive $800 per month at age 65, you will receive $640 (about 80%) by electing to receive benefits at age 62.

Take the $640 per month and put it into an investment that pays 8%. In three years when you turn 65, you will have over $26,000. Then if, at age 65, you wish to start using your Social Security, you will still be receiving your $640 (increased, of course, because of inflation). In addition, you can start drawing interest on the $26,000 you saved at 8%, which is about $170 per month, giving you a total that is higher than the $800 you would have received by waiting. What's more, you have an extra $25,000 of principal in your pocket for your retirement savings! Can you imagine the difference if you earned 9% on your money? Or if you compounded Social Security benefits until you were seventy? I like the fact that the money would be in my pocket, not in Uncle Sam's. Remember, however, that risk is involved whenever you are investing. You might or might not be able to earn 8%. Make certain you are absolutely clear about your decision.

Consider for a moment that you may need the money immediately and cannot invest it until you reached age 65. Again, you will be receiving almost $25,000 over those three years, and it would take about fifteen years to make it up with the extra $160 per month you would have received by waiting until you were 65. Assuming you did no investing whatsoever, I suppose there is an argument for waiting to take the money until you reach age 65, but I would not wait just because I did not need the money. I would rather have the $25,000 than leave it in the good hands of Social Security.

Finally, when you read the chapter discussing Medicaid planning, you will find an argument for showing lower monthly income.

THE RETIREMENT INCOME TEST FOR SOCIAL SECURITY

AT WHAT AMOUNT OF INCOME WILL YOUR SOCIAL SECURITY BENEFITS BE REDUCED?

Many people ask, "If I keep working, will I receive Social Security benefits and will my benefits be taxed?"

If your income exceeds the Social Security earnings limitations, your benefits may be reduced. The earnings limitation test applies until you reach age 70, and afterward

Social Security benefits are usually not reduced. (After age 70 you are entitled to earn any amount of money without any benefits being reduced.) If you earn more than the allowable amount set by the earnings limitation test, Social Security will reduce your benefits.

In 1993, if you are between the ages of 65 and 69, your income limit is $10,560 (under 65 is $7,680). Every year these amounts increase. Under the age of 65 they increase by $1.00 for every $2.00 you earn of the earnings limitation during the year. If you are between the ages of 65 and 69, the reduction in Social Security benefits is $1.00 for every $3.00 of excess earnings.

For instance, if you are currently 65 years of age, and earn $20,000 per year from your employer, you are allowed to receive $10,200 in Social Security before your benefits are reduced. In this case you are vulnerable to the amount of $9,800 (subtract $10,200 from $20,000). If you reduce that amount by $1.00 for every $3.00 of excess earnings, it equates approximately to a 33% reduction in your benefits. Now, 33% of $9,800 equals $3,266. That is the amount your Social Security benefits will be reduced.

In calculating your total earnings for this income test, it is important to note the many sources of income that are not included in the earnings limitation test: pension pay, dividends and interest for investments, possible annuities or certain trust funds, rental income and lottery winnings. Payments for certain tax-exempt trust funds such as profit sharing purchases or annuities may also be included. *Note: This is not a complete list and you should consult with a Social Security expert regarding questions on this matter.*

TAXATION OF SOCIAL SECURITY BENEFITS

Most people enjoy tax-free Social Security benefits. However, after your income exceeds a certain amount, the benefits you receive will be taxed. In 1993, up to half of the benefits you earn can be subject to tax. You can earn $25,000 before being taxed if you are single and $32,000 for a married couple filing a joint return. This is subject to change.

Almost all sources of income are used to calculate a total income. This includes pensions, income dividends, employment, half your Social Security benefits and *Tax-Exempt Bond Interest.* This is a critical item, because many people invest in tax-free bonds with absolutely no knowledge that income from tax-free bonds is added into your gross income for Social Security benefits. In fact, in the upcoming chapter about taxes I will argue that tax-free instruments are not for everyone.

Once the total income is figured, Social Security then uses whichever amount is smaller – the half over the allowed threshold, or the half the Social Security benefits paid.

CONSIDER THIS EXAMPLE OF A MARRIED COUPLE:

Pensions, Dividends and Interest	$40,000
Tax-Free Bond Interest	5,000
One-Half Social Security Benefits	+ 7,000
TOTAL:	$52,000
Allowed Amount	- 32,000
Excess Amount	$20,000
Smaller of the Two Amounts:	
One-Half Excess Amount	$10,000
One-Half of Social Security	$ 7,000

In this case $7,000 is the amount of the Social Security benefits you will have to include on your tax return under adjusted gross income – the item on which your taxes are based. And current legislation is proposed to tax up to 85% of your benefits!

SOCIAL SECURITY BENEFITS AFTER THE FIRST DEATH

Although many restrictions apply, if the widow(er) is over age 60 and not entitled to a Social Security benefit higher than the deceased spouse, the survivor files an application for widow(er) benefits. If the couple was married for at least nine months prior to the death (exceptions apply), the surviving spouse will be entitled to benefits. One possible exception would be if the spouse died accidentally, in which case the nine month period is waived.

The widow(er) is entitled to receive reduced Social Security benefits between the ages of 60-64, or the survivor may wait until age 65 and receive the full retirement benefits. The amount would equal 100% of what the deceased spouse would have received. However, if the widow(er) takes the reduced payment before 65, he or she is not entitled to the full benefit at age 65.

The formula is as follows: The benefit is reduced by 19/40 of 1% for each month that the widow(er) is under age 65 when the benefits begin. So, check your formula – if you take the benefits at 62, you should be receiving roughly 82.9%.

If the widow(er) remarries after the age of 60 the benefit should not be reduced.

If the survivor is entitled to Social Security as well as the deceased's benefits, the survivor would have a make a choice as to which one to take. You cannot get both.

CHAPTER 5

Your Individual Retirement Account:
Rules and Guidelines

Originally *Individual Retirement Accounts* were allowed to provide a tax break for someone trying to plan for retirement. Probably about the time our lawmakers figured out that Social Security just would not provide enough, they devised an incentive for people to save their own money for retirement.

The incentive was the IRA. You could contribute $2,000 ($2,250 for a non-working spouse and a working spouse) per year provided you earned an active income over $2,000 per year. The advantage was that you were able to deduct $2,000 from your gross income to arrive at your adjusted gross income. In effect, this lowered your income by $2,000. In addition, the funds accumulated tax-deferred (with some restrictions) until you withdrew it.

If you withdrew the money prior to age 59 1/2 you would be faced with a 10% penalty from the IRS on the money you withdrew, plus the amount would show up as income and it would be taxed at your ordinary tax rates.

Although not important to this discussion, the IRA has had many overhauls and has changed dramatically since it was originally introduced. The important point to remember is that if you have no active earned income, you can no longer contribute to an IRA. If you do have active earned income and don't need the money, the IRA is still a great savings vehicle.

WHERE TO KEEP IT -- HOW TO HOLD IT

Many people distribute their IRAs in several locations. I think there is nothing wrong with this practice, as long as you are not paying excess fees. If you like the flexibility of investing your IRA in several places – stocks, bonds, Ginnie Maes, CDs and mutual funds, I would advise finding one IRA custodial company that will hold all your assets. This should reduce custodial fees, and allow you to enjoy one, consolidated statement. Most custodians are insured against fraud and bankruptcy.

Many people ask me if they can keep their IRAs at several locations, or are they required to withdraw a little amount from each IRA. The answer is no. An easier tactic is to total your IRAs and withdraw the amount required from just one or two accounts.

TAKING DISTRIBUTIONS

At age 70 1/2, you must start to take a minimum distribution. You may begin taking benefits without penalty at age 59 1/2, but you are *required* to begin taking them at age 70 1/2.

Technically, you must begin taking distributions no later than April 1 of the year following the year you turn 70 1/2. In subsequent years you must take the distribution by December 31 of each year.

THERE ARE SEVERAL WAYS TO TAKE IRA DISTRIBUTIONS WHICH INCLUDE:

1. Take a lump sum.

2. Purchase an annuity with the IRA proceeds.

3. Take yearly payouts of equal amounts over the fixed term of your life expectancy or of you and your beneficiary, or...

4. Take yearly payouts over your life expectancy, with the life expectancy to be recalculated every year. (The life expectancy recalculation method generally provides for smaller distribution amount since the life expectancy increases with each passing year.) This would be the best option if you want to take the least amount out as possible.

LUMP SUM

Obviously this is usually not recommended since it provides for the highest tax. Remember, when money comes out of an IRA it is considered income in that year.

ANNUITY PURCHASE

If you so choose, you may take your IRA and buy an annuity. This is what many seniors do instead of taking a lump sum from a company-sponsored pension plan upon retirement.

The nice thing about this method is you know that you can never outlive your IRA savings. Of course, the negative is the income may not live up to your expectations. Once this option is selected, it can never be changed. You no longer have any access to your principal. Now you must be satisfied with only the income. You also must be sure to pick a solid annuity carrier to avoid losing your money.

EQUAL PAYMENTS OVER A FIXED TERM

This method spreads your payments over your life expectancy, as determined by IRS tables. If you have nominated a beneficiary, the payments can be made over a fixed period based on your joint life expectancies.

So, what would you do if you wanted a very low required IRA payment? Make a young person (such as your grandchild) your IRA beneficiary.

YEARLY RECALCULATION

This method probably would allow you the smallest payments because your life expectancy becomes larger as the years pass. (Our life span lengthens.)

Note: If you do not choose any other method, this method will be elected by default.

The tables and the rules are all set by IRS guidelines. The rules to calculate life expectancy change depending on your beneficiary, as a result they get somewhat complex. The following would be an example.

HOW TO CALCULATE THE REQUIRED MINIMUM DISTRIBUTION

STEP ONE -- DETERMINE YOUR NET IRA BALANCE

1. Add up all the IRAs and determine the *Fair Market Value.*
2. Add the amount of any distributions taken from your IRAs in the current year. If you turned 70 in the current year, simply use "0."
3. Subtract (2) from (1) and write the result. This is your *Net IRA Balance* used in calculating your *Required Minimum Distribution.*

STEP TWO -- DETERMINE YOUR LIFE EXPECTANCY FACTOR

Either use Section 1, 2 or 3:

SECTION 1: If your beneficiary is your spouse, complete this part; if not, move to 2. Your distributions are probably based on a joint life expectancy. Every year you must recalculate your life expectancy based on both ages. To determine your joint life expectancy, call the IRS for their pamphlet that includes a *Current Mortality Table.*

SECTION 2: Use if you do not have a spouse as your beneficiary.

If you do not have a spouse, your life expectancy will not be factored on a joint life basis. Use the IRA *Single Mortality Table* to calculate your life expectancy factor.

SECTION 3: Use this section if you have taken required distributions for previous years and have not recalculated your life expectancy every year. Subtract 1 (the number one) from the life expectancy you used to calculate your minimum distribution. Write down the result.

STEP THREE: DETERMINE YOUR REQUIRED DISTRIBUTION

1. Enter your net IRA balance from Step One.
2. Enter your corresponding life expectancy factor from Step Two.
3. Divide One by Two. Enter the result.
4. Enter any mandatory withdrawals taken in 1993.
5. Subtract 4 from 3 and the result should equal your 1993 required minimum distribution.

WHEN INCOME IS PAID

When you receive the income for the IRA, chances are the taxes will automatically be withheld. You can choose not to have any taxes withheld, but you must request this in writing on form W-9 and specify that you are not subject to back-up withholding. Do not wait until a withdrawal is made, since it is not easy to change the procedure. The withdrawals made from your IRA will be considered ordinary income and should be reported as such on your tax forms. Any distributions you receive from your IRA will be reported on the 1099-R tax form, which you will receive along with the Internal Revenue Service, so be sure they match.

If you have made any non-deductible contributions to your IRA, you are required to file Form 8606 with your tax return when you take a distribution. This form can be obtained from your tax advisor or the IRS.

IRA TRANSFERS AND ROLLOVERS

If you have an IRA, and for any reason wish to change the custodian holding the investment, you can do this in two ways, a transfer or a rollover.

An *IRA Transfer* is when you never actually take possession of the money. Instead, you instruct the new IRA custodian (the one to which you are transferring funds), to transfer the funds. They will notify the current custodian and have the funds transferred. You are allowed to transfer IRAs as often as you wish.

For example: Your IRA is held at a bank and you now wish to have the IRA in a mutual fund. The mutual fund will provide you with the various transfer forms. You send them back to the fund (or to your advisor), and they will complete the transfer.

An *IRA Rollover* is slightly different. This involves taking possession of the funds. Using the same scenario, you wish to liquidate your funds from the bank, but want to actually take possession of the money. The bank will give you the money after filling out an IRA distribution form (make sure you tell them *not* to withhold taxes). Once they give you the funds, you will have 60 days in which to roll over the funds into another IRA. If you do not roll the funds over, you will be obligated to pay income tax on the full amount you received.

When you roll over funds you will receive a 1099-R tax form from the previous custodian. You will not owe taxes as long as you prove the funds were reinvested into another IRA within 60 days. If you do an IRA rollover the custodian will usually make the check payable to you. You should deposit the funds into your checking account, and be sure you write a check for the exact amount your received to the new custodian within 60 days.

An IRA rollover is only allowed *once per year.*

Much talk has been centered around the 20% withholding tax. This new tax is applicable if you are rolling over a pension or other qualified plan to an IRA. If you take possession of the funds (from the pension), even though you are still planning to roll the benefits into an IRA, an automatic 20% withholding tax will be levied. Personally, I feel this tax is a waste and a way to prey on those who do not understand rollover rights.

It is very simple to avoid this 20% withholding tax. All you do is select a *Direct Rollover* of your benefits. In other words, instruct your pension to send the funds directly to the new custodian of your IRA. The new custodian may be a bank, a mutual fund company, brokerage account, or a self-directed IRA custodian.

One benefit of a self-directed IRA custodian is the flexibility of investing your funds in practically any investment that you are legally allowed to own in an IRA. You may choose to buy stocks, bonds, real estate or mutual funds. However, be sure to obtain the proper forms before initiating the rollover process.

WHAT TO DO WITH YOUR SPOUSE`S IRA AFTER YOUR SPOUSE`S DEATH

After the death of the spouse, the survivor has two primary options, providing the surviving spouse is the primary beneficiary.

1.   Roll the funds over into the survivor`s IRA

Tax laws allow the surviving spouse to rollover the decedent's IRA funds. The result will be an IRA in the survivor's name and the avoidance of probate. Since the funds were rolled into the surviving spouse's IRA, no taxes are owed until the spouse withdraws the funds from his/her IRA. Note that only spouses can rollover IRAs. A father or mother, for example, may not roll an IRA into a child's name.

2.   Request the full proceeds of the IRA

Provided the spouse is the primary beneficiary, the spouse can request the full proceeds of the decedent's IRA. Again, this would result in no probate and immediate access to the money. However, this would be considered a full IRA distribution and all the taxes on the full proceeds would be owed during that year.

PROPER WORDING OF AN IRA

Chances are, if you have not already created an IRA, you will not be creating one now. If you are already retired and have no active income, you are no longer eligible to create an IRA. If you do have an IRA, you should check the paperwork to make sure everything is in order.

Confirm that the name is correctly spelled with a current address and birth date. Even more important, make certain the beneficiaries are correct. Ideally, you would want your spouse as the primary beneficiary and your trust as the secondary, or contingent, beneficiary. If you do not have a trust then decide who you would want to receive your assets in the event both you and your spouse die simultaneously. If your IRA does not go to your spouse, or into a trust, and you do not have proper beneficiary named, the IRA may go through probate. Likewise, if you are unmarried and do not properly name a beneficiary, your assets may go through probate. Don't let this happen. By nominating a beneficiary this asset can avoid probate. So be prepared in advance!

CHAPTER 6

Taxes: How To Reduce
and Avoid Them

The sad truth is that mature Americans often pay a higher percentage of taxes than any other segment of the population. Technically, the income is supposed to be lower than when you were working. But if you total your Social Security income, retirement income, and dividends, it adds up. If you are actively investing and doing a good job, that may increase your taxes. Also, the deductions of the average retiree are usually few and far between. In most cases you cannot itemize your deductions, can't deduct dependents and have no business writeoffs, so your tax bracket often turns out to be higher than you expected.

When you retire, you may overlook paying taxes in your financial plan. Even when creating your financial plan, very seldom do people compute taxes properly. The truth is that taxes, over time, are on an upward trend. Seniors have very little means by which to shelter their estates from taxes, resulting sometimes in their being in a higher tax bracket than when they were working full time.

In addition to income taxes, you could be subject to capital gains taxes on the sale of an investment, property taxes, gift taxes, and even estate taxes or death taxes after you pass away. Do you ever wonder with all these taxes why the United States is running at such a deficit? I know I do!

All in all, taxes are quite a pain. The mature American must find every legal means to reduce his or her tax burden. The less you pay in taxes, the higher your true return on investments and the more conservative your portfolio. The following are a few ideas to reduce your tax burden.

To reduce income taxes, either you have to avoid the tax, reduce the tax or conceal your income. We will deal only with the first two options.

WAYS TO AVOID TAXES

TAX-FREE MUNICIPAL BONDS

You can purchase tax-free municipal bonds as individual bonds or through a mutual fund. The income from municipal bonds issued in the state you live are completely exempt from all federal and state taxes.

What is important is that although these might be a tax-free investment, you must figure out if they will pay you more money than a taxable investment (after taxes). If I were to ask you which is better, a tax-free bond paying 5% or a taxable bond paying 7% (assuming both bonds are AAA-rated and insured), what would your response be?

THE EASIEST WAY TO COMPUTE YOUR TAXABLE EQUIVALENT YIELD IS TO:
(ASSUME WE ARE USING A TAX-FREE BOND YIELDING 5%)

1. Determine your federal and state tax bracket. For this exercise, let's assume it is 31%.
2. Subtract your tax bracket from 100 (100 - 31 = 69).
3. Divide the tax-free return by 69 (5 ÷ 69 = .072, or 7.2%).

With a taxable equivalent yield of greater than 7.2%, it becomes clear that 5% tax free is better than 7% taxable (provided our assumption of a 31% tax bracket is correct). It would take a taxable equivalent yield of 7.2% to beat a tax-free yield of 5%.

Let's assume that all you know is the taxable return (in this case 7%) and you want to determine the tax-free equivalent yield. Multiply your tax bracket reciprocal (assume it is 31%) by the taxable return (69 x .07 = 4.8%) to get the tax-free equivalent yield of 4.8%. This means that any tax-free yield of greater than 4.8% or better is superior to a 7% taxable rate of return.

When analyzing tax-free bonds, be sure to take their quality into account – some are better then others. Also, be sure you know if the bond is tax free for both state and federal purposes. If it is not free of state tax that means that the bond was probably issued in another state. Nothing is wrong with this as long as the yield is higher than the double tax-free one, or the one that is fully taxable.

THE MAIN PROBLEMS WITH TAX-FREE BONDS ARE:

1. They are more difficult to analyze since they are not all AAA-rated and insured.

2. Although the interest is tax-free, the income is still calculated in your gross income to determine if your Social Security benefits will be taxed. Many people don't realize that this tax-free income affects the taxability of your Social Security. In addition, you might be subject to the ALTERNATIVE MINIMUM TAX which is a tax everyone must pay.

3. In many cases these bonds are long-term in nature and must be held until maturity to get your principal back in periods of rising interest because the principal value of a bond drops in an environment of rising interest rates.

GOVERNMENT BONDS, TREASURY NOTES AND BILLS, ZERO COUPON GOVERNMENT BONDS

These issues are direct obligations of the United States Government and are free from all state tax. Although not usually the main reason to purchase one of these investments, if your state income tax rate is high, this could be a factor in deciding if the investment suits your needs.

Many people have been accumulating and investing in *Series EE Bonds.* The benefit of EE bonds is that they are issued at a discount and mature to their face value. You may defer all the tax until you cash in the bond. The problem is that when you cash the bond, you have to pay tax on the gain all the way back to your original purchase price. Obviously this can cause you a tax problem. The only way to avoid this situation is by converting the bonds into *Series HH Bonds.* But now you have to pay taxes every year on the interest, and the interest paid is usually substantially lower.

CAPITAL GAINS OFFSET CAPITAL LOSSES

If you have a gain on a stock or any security and are not selling it just because of the capital gain, find an investment in your portfolio on which you are willing to take a loss to offset that gain. Don't sell the investment just because it is down. However, if you think the investment is down and is going to stay down for a long period of time, consider selling the investment for the loss. The loss will offset the capital gain from your stock.

In addition, you are allowed (after the 1986 Tax Reform Act), up to $3,000 per year in losses to be used against any source of income. This means you can offset a loss from an investment from income sources other than investments.

Another excellent technique is to take year-end losses. If you can sell something at the end of the year for a loss, but like the investment, sell the stock at the end of the year and buy it back 31 days later. Be fairly sure that the price of that investment will be the same 31 days later, or you might end up missing out on the appreciation of an investment simply to avoid the taxes. But be careful. If you buy a stock back within 30 days after the sell, you will be in violation of the *Wash Sale Rule.* If you are in violation, you will not be able to deduct your loss.

A similar technique is called *Tax Swapping.* If you own a stock that is down, and you see another stock you would consider that will do better than the stock you currently own, you may consider a swap. You would sell the stock (and incur a capital loss), then purchase the new stock.

The benefit could allow you to upgrade your portfolio and generate tax losses at the same time. The capital losses generated from a swap would directly offset realized capital gains, which would have been taxed at the same rate as your tax bracket. In addition, you are allowed to take $3,000 of the losses and offset it against any income.

MATCHING PASSIVE INCOME TO PASSIVE LOSSES

If you have passive income investments, find an investment that generates a passive loss to offset the passive income. Passive income can only be offset by passive losses and vice versa. A typical investment that might throw off passive income (or losses) could include limited partnerships or perhaps rental real estate.

For example, if you have rental real estate that generates passive income, find a type of investment that, although it might be appreciating and doing well, throws off passive losses. The result would be the income from the real estate tax free, to the extent of your passive income losses. You would also be able to use passive losses from another viable investment that could have gone wasted. Many tax credit programs in senior housing, or low-income housing, generate passive losses in addition to the credit.

USE PRINCIPAL FOR INCOME

Almost regardless of who is talking, you'll hear, "Never use your principal – only income from investments." My question is, "Why not?"

If you simply take income from all your investments, you are probably not allowing yourself to make more money by *Dollar-Cost Averaging.* You will be receiving many checks, some not very large and you are paying taxes on all your dividends (unless they are from tax-free bonds).

Answer this: If you had $100,000 separated into three separate accounts, each paying 8% ($8,000 per year), would you simply take the income from all three accounts, or take the income and principal from two accounts (to equal $8,000), and allow one to compound?

Let's analyze the two scenarios:

In scenario one, you have three accounts, each yielding about 8%, giving you $8,000 per year in taxable income. In five years you will still have the $100,000 since you never touched principal, and you paid the full tax on your income.

In scenario two, again you have three accounts of $33,330 each paying 8%. To maintain the 8% per year from two of the accounts, you take the income from the two accounts equaling $5,330. In addition you withdraw $2,670 worth of principal every year to give you the total $8,000. Your two accounts will be worth $53,310 in five years. Now the third account has been dollar-cost averaging every month earning an average of 8% per year over the last five years. The account started with $33,300 and is now worth $50,000 as a result of successful dollar-cost averaging, and allowing the account to compound without withdrawing proceeds. This process is most effective using an annuity, an IRA, or other tax-advantaged investment to avoid taxation on the compounded funds.

Now your account total is worth over $103,000 (more than you had to start), and you paid significantly less taxes since you only withdrew $5,330 per year worth of income. The money you withdrew from your principal is not taxed again, only the income is taxed. I see the extra $3,000 as free income that you earned without working harder or taking a risk. It is your hedge against inflation. Plus look at all the tax savings.

I think most investors need a little growth in their portfolio – some more than others (based on your required rate of return). Still, many people argue they cannot afford growth because they need all the income their investments generate. Before you say that, repeat the above exercise using your numbers. Take enough principal to satisfy your income, then find an investment with the probable return you want.

You say you cannot afford growth? With the length of time we are living and at the high costs of living, can you afford to miss any growth?

INVESTING IN NON-INCOME PRODUCING ASSETS

You are reminded throughout this book that you should not be investing until your plan is in place. One point I can't emphasize enough is that if you already have your income covered, and you don't need additional income, minimize the amount you invest in income-producing assets. Income-producing vehicles include: Certificates of deposit, income mutual funds, stocks and stocks with dividends. All of these investments will issue you a 1099 tax statement each year showing the amount of taxable income. In fact, even if you have reinvested the income you receive a 1099. If you have all the income you need, why not invest in vehicles that do not have income?

You can invest in stocks or mutual funds that have only capital gains (hopefully) but no dividends. These are stocks that are more oriented toward growth but after you do your financial plan you will know how much growth you need. Some types of real estate do not offer dividends or income. These might be a wise diversification tool. Annuities defer all your income, so you can invest in guaranteed interest accounts, like CDs, but defer the income until you withdraw the funds. Or, if you like income-type mutual funds, invest inside the annuity to defer all the tax.

If your retirement check and Social Security benefits take care of all living expenses and you still have extra funds, minimize any additional realized income. If you have IRAs or annuities, you could invest in all the dividend-paying, interest-bearing accounts you want and defer the tax. This would be opposed to keeping the money liquid and receiving a 1099 tax statement every year. If you still have more money that you want to keep liquid, invest in mutual funds and stocks outside the annuity and in IRAs that do not pay dividends. I know this strategy sounds reversed, but think about it. You have just constructively reduced your exposure to current taxable income without changing the amount of risk to which you are exposing your portfolio.

TAX DEFERRAL

If you analyze the sections and benefits related to tax deferral, it is quite apparent that tax deferral is truly one of the best ways to compound income and delay taxation. On any tax-deferred investments (annuities, IRA, etc.), the 1099 tax form shows no current income, so there is no tax to report. Social Security benefits are not impacted and income is thereby lowered as a result of the income not realized by this investment. However, your money still continues to compound and at a faster rate than if taxes were taken out every year. If you invest in tax-free instruments such as municipal bonds and bond funds, and are reinvesting the money, why not earn a higher interest rate in, for instance, a government bond fund but in a tax-deferred vehicle like an annuity? You still have the advantage of investing in a conservative fund, only now you can defer all the tax.

Remember that the interest from tax-free bonds and bond funds is still counted as gross income for Social Security tax purposes. If your income (and age) exceed the limit allowed by Social Security, you will owe taxes. In tax-deferred accounts, thousands of dollars could be generating and appreciating for you. But until you actually withdraw the money, none of it is considered current income.

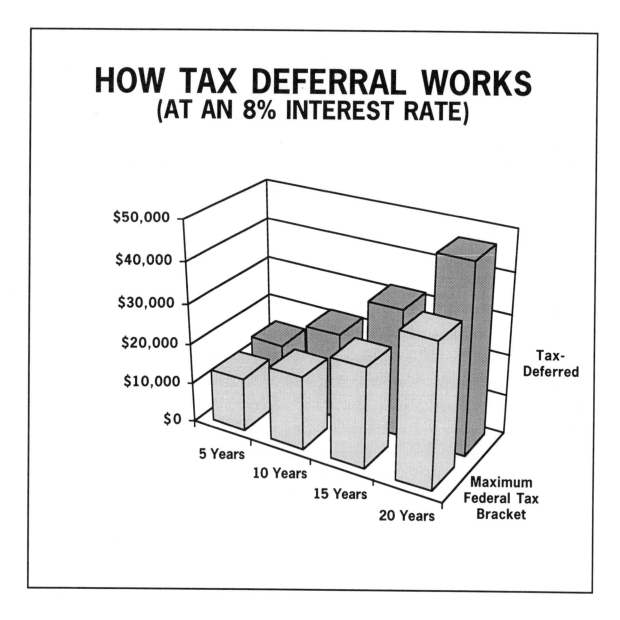

HOW TAX DEFERRAL WORKS
(AT AN 8% INTEREST RATE)

Even if you are reinvesting the money from a tax-free bond fund, you still receive a Tax Form 1099 and have to claim it as current income every year.

Research this thoroughly and give serious consideration to the merits of investments such as tax-deferred annuities (see the Annuity section).

``ANNUITIZE`` AN ANNUITY

If you have an annuity that is in the accumulation stage, and are ready to start taking income but cannot bear the extra tax, consider *Annuitizing the Annuity.* The advantages would include higher income than similar investments, steady income guaranteed for a set number of years with part of the income being tax free. The biggest disadvantage would be loss of access to your principal. Your principal is no longer yours; you relinquish all rights to it. If you opt for this strategy, make sure the company you choose is very conservative and enjoys the highest industry ratings. (You will find more about annuities under Types of Investments.)

CAPITAL GAINS -- SECTION 121

For people over the age of 55 who would like to sell their homes, but want to avoid paying taxes, use of *Section 121* may be the answer. Section 121 will allow you to write off up to $125,000 of a gain you might have to pay on the sale of your personal residence. As always, strict rules apply. Among the major ones: (1) You are required to have lived in your home for the last three out of five years, (2) neither you nor your spouse has previously used the Section 121 and, (3) you must be over 55, with the house being your principal residence.

REDUCING YOUR TAXES

The previous section discussed ways *to avoid* paying taxes. The following will discuss ways *to reduce* your taxes.

CHARITABLE GIFTS

Any time you make a charitable gift, you are allowed to take a deduction (or credit) on your tax return. The amount you can deduct will vary depending on the gift and type of charity. Be sure to document all gifts.

If you make gifts of personal property such as furniture or clothing, you can deduct the *Fair Market Value* of what is given to a charity. Make sure you ask the charity for a receipt showing the value of the donated items. If you cannot obtain a receipt, then keep of an itemized list of the items you donated, the recipient's name and address, the date and place of the donation, and your estimated fair market value of each item.

If you are planning to gift property, it makes sense to give appreciated assets such as stock or real estate since you will not have to recognize the gain. However, the recipient will ultimately have to pay tax on the gain.

In addition to charitable gifting, many people donate time for charitable work. If you have expenses associated with this work and can prove the services have been provided to a qualified organization, you may be able to deduct these expenses. You have a choice when considering travel expenses by deducting the actual out-of-pocket costs for gas and oil, or using the standard rate of 12 cents per mile. Tolls and parking may also be included.

To avoid capital gains tax, many people create *Charitable Trusts* (see Charitable Trust section). You can put a highly appreciated asset in an *Irrevocable Charitable Trusts* (the asset can be stock, real estate or most assets), then once the asset is in the charitable trust, it can be sold and the entire proceeds of the sale can go into an investment to pay you income. You would receive a charitable deduction for the gift, and would enjoy income on the full proceeds, not the proceeds less any capital gains tax you would have otherwise paid. Plus, if structured correctly, you can show part of the income coming back as return of principal to avoid paying taxes on the entire amount of income.

As discussed in many of the estate planning chapters, you can always gift property or investments to avoid paying a taxable gain (although your beneficiaries might have to pay), or you have the option of creating a life estate.

RENTAL INCOME

If you have the tolerance, patience and time, rental real estate can be a method of making money and reducing taxes. But don't fool yourself into thinking it is anything other than intensive, hands-on management. You will deal with vacancies, irresponsible tenants, repairs, maintenance, advertising and inconvenience.

However, if you can purchase rental property and meet specific criteria, you can offset the rental losses against your ordinary income up to $25,000. Your income must be lower than a certain amount, you must not be in the business of rental real estate or property management, and usually you can only offset losses from a rental to ordinary income on the first rental. If you can show losses, fit the criteria, don't mind the work, and think the rental property will appreciate faster then your true losses, then this is a consideration.

START A BUSINESS

Nowhere is it written that once you retire you can't start a side business. Obviously you will intend to make a profit one day, but in the meantime, the costs of starting the business are high enough to itemize your income tax deductions, which opens the door for taking additional deductions you may now have but cannot use without itemizing.

For instance, say you have been a handyman for many years and have often helped friends and relatives for nominal charges. Now you decide to do this as a part-time business. You can itemize many deductions such as part of your car payment, gasoline, an office in your home, tools, an accountant, an additional phone line and supplies. Obviously strict rules apply to taking any of these deductions, and you may be more likely to be audited, but, again, work the numbers. If they work in your favor you might want to give it a try.

Since you are self-employed (if you have any extra income that you don't need) you can start your own *Simplified Employee Pension (SEP)* and deduct monies you put away in your retirement account.

HOME MORTGAGE

Most people say, "I can't wait until my mortgage is paid." And I always ask, "Why?"

Once again, my reasoning is not conventional, and many people find this to be extremely unorthodox, but in certain market cycles, this practice could have merit.

Let's analyze this situation:

Assume you obtain a thirty-year, fixed-rate mortgage at 8%. And assume you are confident (based on investments available, your risk posture, and portfolio track record) that your investments will earn 10%. If that is the case, why not borrow money at 8%, (through a mortgage) and receive a deduction on all of the interest portion of the mortgage (which is the vast majority in the first several years), and reinvest the money at 10%? You can take the money you receive from the mortgage and place half into an account to pay the monthly payment, and put the other half in a mutual fund inside an annuity to grow tax-deferred. Work the numbers so that you have an account that pays the mortgage payment for you – use a direct deposit. Do not worry about using principal, because you are taking the second account and growing it. Now you are making money on borrowed money, and receiving a very attractive deduction on your mortgage!

If, at a later date, you change your mind and don't want the mortgage, or if your investments aren't earning enough to justify the loan, pay it off. After all, it's not like you don't have the funds – you just redirected them. Be careful about your choices of investments since you cannot afford to lose this money.

Home equity loans also enjoy interest deductions. Use one if you need it. If you plan to buy a new car, use the *Equity Line of Credit* to pay for the car. You will receive the interest deduction off your taxes, and a lower interest rate than you would have from a bank or dealership. However, if the interest rate on the equity line of credit is higher then what you make on your investments, consider paying for the car in cash.

Borrowing money is not so bad if you have enough money to pay off the loan, ***and*** if you can make money on the borrowed money.

TAX CREDITS

Despite popular opinion, viable *Tax Credits* do exist. Different sections of the tax code allow for different types of credits. If you meet the criteria and qualify, credits could exist in select areas: oil and gas investments, low-income housing, senior housing, and historic housing. A potential negative is that you, an individual, probably do want to start a business in these areas to get the credit.

The most popular way to receive the credits is through some type of a *Limited Partnership.* Before any investing, especially in a limited partnership, do a lot of homework. Never invest in a limited partnership without reading the *Prospectus,* knowing the fees (sometimes as high as 20% front-load), and studying in great detail the track record (usually somewhere in the back of the prospectus). See how many programs the sponsor has completed (actually returned money back to the investor) and what return was received. How may actual credits did prior investors receive? Ask if it is being bought for cash or through leverage. Only after you are satisfied with all the answers should you consider investing in a tax credit program.

Here's the way these tax credits work: Whatever credit you receive is deducted from the bottom line of what you would have owed as a tax liability. In other words, if you owe $5,000 in taxes, but received $2,000 in tax credits, you will owe only $3,000 in taxes.

Many people were soured on tax credits after the *1986 Tax Reform Act.* Several partnerships were structured to take advantage of the tax credits being offered without any consideration for the actual merits of a particular investment. Therefore, when

Congress took away the tax credits, many of these programs went bankrupt. *Always invest in the economic benefits first, look at the tax-credits as a bonus.* The credit being offered for low-income or senior housing shows a great deal of evidence that, even if they do not continue offering the credit, prior investors will be allowed to continue the tax credit.

ADDITIONAL TAXES

There are also other taxes that must be taken into consideration.

GIFT TAXES

A gift of any type of asset (property, cash or securities) valued at over $10,000 to a single person in a given year must be reported. However, gifts that pay for medical or educational expenses do *not* need to be reported. Furthermore, if you are the recipient of the gift you are not required to report it although you will have to report the income that is generated by the gift.

Gifting can be an excellent method as long as you have time to plan and are absolutely sure you will never need the money once you have gifted it. Once it's gone – it's gone.

SALES TAX/STATE INCOME TAX

When mature Americans retire, one of the first questions they ask is "Where should we retire or have our second home?"

Frequently overlooked, is the *State Sales Tax* and *Income Tax Ratio* of your potential new state of residence. If your estate is going to have a difficult time staying above water you might want to seriously consider living in a state that has no sales tax or very low sales tax or income tax. These taxes can be far more devastating than people realize. If you are paying an extra 7% per year in taxes because of where you live, you might want to consider relocating for your retirement years.

ESTATE TAX

Arguably, the *Federal Estate Tax* is one of the highest and most usurious tax rates. This tax ranges anywhere from 37% to 55% In addition, if your state charges an estate tax as well, that will be added to your tax burden.

It's important to note that the estate does not begin to be taxed until it reaches a value of $600,000; estates valued under $600,000 are not affected. However, if you give away large assets during your lifetime, this will likely count against your one-time exclusion of $600,000, and thereby reducing the death benefit.

For example, assume your estate is worth $900,000. Let's say part of it is comprised of stock worth $200,000. Before your death, you gift the stock worth $200,000 to your son. Subsequently, you pass away. Usually, that $200,000 gift will be deducted from your one-time $600,000 exclusion, leaving you with a $400,000 exclusion upon death. In this case your estate upon death is worth $700,000, you do not owe taxes on $400,000 leaving you vulnerable to estate taxes of $300,000.

If your estate owes taxes the Internal Revenue Service demands payment within nine months or it will generously liquidate assets in order for you to pay the tax. As you must know by now, the IRS is not gracious. If the estate consists mostly of real estate, you may have to liquidate property at unfavorable economic times, resulting in distress or fire-sale prices. So the question remains, how to reduce estate taxes? Following is a summary of strategies.

A REVOCABLE LIVING TRUST

If you are married, you and your spouse can create a revocable living trust with the A/B provisions (successor/survivor, exemption trust, or any of the other various names under which it is known). The objective would be to separate the estate into two separate parts giving each spouse their own exemption currently worth $600,000. So, effectively, the estate, under current law, would be protected up to $1,200,000 before the estate taxes would begin.

Note: It's important to point out that there is much talk and even a proposed bill to lower the estate tax exclusion from $600,000 to $200,000 – if this happens, watch out!

GIFTING FUNDS

Many mature Americans gift $10,000 per person per year in order to lower their estate to below the $1,200,000. You are allowed to gift to as many people as you want $10,000 per year before paying estate taxes. In addition, you are allowed to gift almost an unlimited amount of money to grandchildren for educational expenses. Of course, provisions apply, the main one being that the tuition must be paid directly to the educational facility. You are also allowed to gift money for health care reasons over the $10,000 limit.

IRREVOCABLE TRUSTS, FAMILY PARTNERSHIPS, PRIVATE ANNUITIES AND CHARITABLE TRUSTS, "GRITS" AND "GRATS"

All of the above can be viable ways to lower the value of the estate value and receive many benefits. However, when discussing these advanced planning techniques, or whenever you hear the word "irrevocable" you know there will be a serious price to pay for using this type of estate planning tool. Usually the biggest price is the loss of control of your asset. However, you can read the Estate Planning section of this book, or study this topic in more detail if it is of interest to you and your estate. And, by all means, consult an investment professional prior to taking any action.

IRREVOCABLE INSURANCE TRUST

Again, this is discussed in detail in the Estate Reduction section. Basically, you can create a trust and have your beneficiary purchase life insurance through the trust. The advantage is that the proceeds will not be included in your estate, resulting in a gift to the beneficiary which he or she may use to pay the taxes you owe. If you simply buy life insurance, the death benefit will increase the size of your estate.

For instance, if your estate is worth $3,000,000 and you have $1,000,000 of life insurance and you pass away, your estate is really worth $4,000,000. That size of an estate falls in the 55% tax bracket. So, in effect, you are paying $1,000,000 for life insurance, of which Uncle Sam gets almost 55%. Whereas, if this insurance was owned and paid for by a separate entity, your estate would not increase by the amount of the insurance.

If you anticipate that your estate is going to owe taxes, why pay the full amount of the tax? Even if the insurance is expensive, it very often it makes sense to use that technique to avoid spending all your money on taxes. One good way to lower the insurance premium is to purchase what is often referred to as *Second-to-Die*

Insurance. In the case of a married couple, this insurance would not pay after the first death, but after the second death, regardless of who dies first. It's less expensive because the mortality tables of both husband and wife are combined, thus lowering the overall cost. In addition, since many of these policies are placed into a trust, you cannot have access to any of the cash value built up from excess premiums. So find a cheaper policy that does not increase in cash value, thereby further reducing the premium cost.

Let's say you know your estate is going to owe $200,000 in estate taxes and you have exhausted all reasonable options. You can create an irrevocable insurance trust, purchasing insurance for $200,000. We will assume it costs $4,000 per year over a ten-year period, totaling a $40,000 cash outlay. If you die after ten years, your total cash outlay of $40,000 will result in your estate receiving $200,000. That compounds to almost a 17% return, not including the time value of money based on the fact you did not have to pay $40,000 all at once. In this example you have been an excellent money manager and where else could you find a 17% tax-free return?

CONTACTING THE IRS

If you need your tax questions answered, want to order tax forms or an IRS publication, call the IRS. The easiest phone numbers to use include:

Telephone tax assistance	1-800-829-1040
To order publications or forms	1-800-829-3676
Taped tax messages and refund information	1-800-829-4477
For the hearing impaired	1-800-829-4059

SERVICES AVAILABLE FOR SENIORS FROM THE IRS

Finally, you will be glad to know that at least part of your tax dollars are going to a worthy cause. This year seniors can get a special tax package, including the most popular forms used by seniors. The 1040A form is included, and has lines for IRA distributions, pensions, annuities and Social Security benefits. Schedule 1 is for reporting over $400 in interest dividends and Schedule 3 is for computing the tax credit for the elderly and the disabled. If you do not receive this form near tax time, you can call the IRS at...

1-800-829-3676.

In addition, you can call this telephone number to receive a special IRS publication for mature Americans. Ask for the ***Tax Information For Older Americans, Form 554.*** This package offers many helpful hints for senior citizens and reviews recent changes in the tax laws. A great feature is sample tax forms printed in large print for easy reading.

Finally, the IRS offers free tax counseling for anyone age 60 or older. Call the IRS number for the location nearest you.

In 1992 many other benefits became available for mature Americans. The most popular include: Unmarried persons 65 or older do not have to file a federal tax return if their income is less then $6,800. Married individuals filing jointly do not have to file with $11,300 in income if only one spouse is over the age of 65. If both spouses are 65 or older, you do not have to file if your income is lower than $12,000. Anyone 65 years or older is entitled to an extra exemption of $2,300.

You are considered 65 years of age on the day of your birthday. So, if you turn 65 any time during the year you will qualify. These above numbers are for 1992 returns. For future returns consult with the IRS to see the upwardly-indexed numbers.

CHAPTER 7

Investing For Safe Money

In times like these *the only constant is change.* I hope these basic planning techniques will help you maximize your situation. But remember, it is important to keep abreast of new developments as they occur and always refer to your financial plan.

Safe Money is of the utmost importance. People are living longer and in a more expensive world. Our money needs to at the very least maintain its value after taxes and inflation. If you earn 5% on a CD, figure on subtracting about 1.5% for taxes, and then at least 4% for inflation, barely breaking even on your money, or actually losing money. Now that the government is saying inflation is low, I am skeptical. The inflation rate for retired individuals is probably much higher. Costs on travel and leisure alone usually rise more than 10% per year.

I am concerned when I see mature Americans invest all of their savings in stocks and then rely on the market for monthly income and growth. In certain proportions, the stock market has advantages. However, the stock market can lose money as well.

Having all your money in banks, cash or CDs is not always the answer either. The banks pay a low interest rate which often erodes the principal. Sometimes it can be difficult to live off the minimal income CDs provide. You have worked hard for retirement and, if planned properly, you should not be in a position where you have to worry about compromising your lifestyle.

WHEN LOOKING FOR SAFE MONEY, CERTAIN CRITERIA SHOULD BE FOLLOWED. MY CHECK LIST INCLUDES THE FOLLOWING THREE INGREDIENTS:

1. SAFETY
Money should be in either AAA-rated or similar vehicles to minimize risk and avoid wide principal fluctuations.

2. LIQUIDITY
In these economic times money should be liquid enough so that if you needed it you can access it immediately. Buying United States government bond mutual funds might not be the answer because the bonds they are buying usually have maturities greater than 15 years. If rates rise, your share price will probably go down. This money should be kept in short-term vehicles. Investments inside a fund should have a five-year maximum maturity in periods of rising interest rates.

3. COMPETITIVE YIELDS
It is not a matter of choice anymore. If you want to maintain your standard of living, and make money, you have to make at least 2% above interest and taxes.

In other words, if you find an investment that fits the above three criteria, it's worth considering. Remember, 100% of your portfolio should never be in safe money, growth or real estate. It's a solid balance that makes the difference. The balance is derived when you create your financial plan.

Through proper planning and research you can find these types of investments. Before doing any investing, find your required rate of return. If all you need is to earn 7%, enough safe vehicles exist to earn you that 7% and that is where you should be investing. Again, finding that required rate of return is a key part of building your financial plan. I cannot stress enough *that you must have a plan!*

Based on the above information, this is what I recommend:

INVESTMENT POSSIBILITIES

ADJUSTABLE RATE MORTGAGE FUNDS (ARMS)

One very popular vehicle has been the use of *Adjustable Rate Mortgage Funds (ARMs).* These funds typically invest in short-term treasuries and adjustable rate mortgages. The goal of these types of funds is usually the safety of the principal first, with interest secondary. The concept is if interest rates rise, so will the rates on adjustable mortgage and short-term treasuries. Although the yield will not be as high as a government fund, the principal does not fluctuate as much. So, in periods of rising interest rates, these mutual funds are supposed to pay the higher yield more quickly, and principal should not be as affected as with a long-term fund.

I think the popularity of these funds came as the result of fears over rising interest. Most government funds are long-term in nature and will probably suffer share price loss if interest rates rise. Another reason for the popularity of ARMS was to help someone who had always invested in CDs or other guaranteed accounts, to become exposed to investing in a mutual fund, but with a low-risk approach. Either way, they seem to serve a purpose and have found a niche in the market among investors.

GOVERNMENT TRUSTS

You have the choice of where to place your money. Why not directly invest in the United States government and its agencies? Remember, the banks are not in business for free and your deposits are reinvested to earn the banks more money then they will pay you. Your money might be invested in real estate mortgages or short-term Treasury issues and, in turn, you will receive a portion of the rate the bank earns. However, you can take control and invest directly in the same type of short-term investments on your own.

You can invest in short-term pools that buy into securities that are backed by the United States government and its agencies. By pooling your money with others in these types of trusts you can enjoy higher rates in addition to safety. Many of these accounts are reinsured by a reinsurance organization or backed by the security of the U.S. government.

CMOs

In 1983, the introduction of *Collateralized Mortgage Obligations (CMOs)* by the *Federal Home Loan Mortgage Corporation* established a new investment vehicle for investors who were not traditionally involved in the mortgage market. CMOs took regular 30-year mortgages and created obligations comprised of many different classes, technically known as *Traunches.*

Basically, a CMO is like a bond, a debt issue secured by pools of mortgages guaranteed by government agencies (Freddie Mac, Fannie Mae, Ginnie Mae). Although there are private corporations or other agencies that issue securities and call them CMOs, be careful – know the agency that is guaranteeing it before investing in one. Almost all of the government- or agency-backed CMOs will receive an AAA-implied rating.

There are many different types (traunches) of CMOs, so it is easy to find one that fits your exact needs. This could include: Estimated maturity, frequency of interest payments, how fast principal is returned, low minimum investments (sometimes as low as $1,000). CMOs do return principal, so be careful. If you intend on researching CMOs with the possibility of purchasing one you might want to ask the broker to hold all principal in your account. That way you are not receiving both principal and interest and having nothing left after the obligation is paid off.

CMOs can offer many wonderful advantages, including higher interest, for the safety associated with it, short-term maturities, and relative liquidity. However, they can be confusing. You should ask such questions as, "How fast will it pay off?" or "Will it pay me back all of my principal and interest too early?"

Also know how much you are paying per bond, or obligation. Try not to pay over par, or over $1,000 per unit. The cheaper you can get it, the better your yield will be.

SHORT-TERM GLOBAL GOVERNMENT BONDS

It is amazing that government bonds of sovereign nations have outperformed United States bonds almost every year for the past 15 years. Many investors don't realize that other leading nations have superior credit ratings to the United States because they don't carry the debt the U.S. does.

Investing in short-term global bonds (from Canada, Switzerland, Italy, England or Australia), will pay you a much higher interest rate even after the exchange conversion. Some are currently paying more than 8%. By investing only short-term, you have minimal principal risk and can sell the bonds as your discretion. Now, more than ever, could be the right time to invest in short-term world government income mutual funds. With international bond rates following the United States in their downward movements, you can take advantage of a good yield while it lasts.

SHORT-TERM NATIONAL MUNICIPAL BONDS

If you need the tax-free status, there are national *Municipal Bond Trusts* that invest only in institutional quality bonds issued by municipalities all over the nation. Currently they pay as high as 6% and are federally tax-free. That equates to a taxable yield of over 8%. The maturities of these bonds are usually under five years and they are completely liquid.

CONVERTIBLE BONDS

Americans are living longer than ever before, unfortunately at much higher costs. It is for that reason we need to make sure that at least some part of your portfolio is increasing in value. However, if you need income, that is a bit more difficult to do. One excellent alternative is *Convertible Bonds.*

A convertible bond will offer steady income with the chance for appreciation. Technically you can buy a bond with a stated interest rate. However, if the company's stock appreciates, you have the right to convert your bond into shares of stock, at a stated conversion price. As a result, you will receive the appreciated shares, at an previously agreed-upon lower price. If the stock does not appreciate, you keep the bond and continue earning interest until the bond matures.

Obviously you must do extensive research to make certain you have a good bond, a stock that will appreciate, and a safe company standing behind them. But, if after researching the offering, you are satisfied with the results, this type of security offers many advantages.

TAX-DEFERRED, INSURED, GUARANTEED ANNUITIES

Many fixed annuities offer AAA ratings with different maturity dates and with all earnings tax deferred. These investments have no principal fluctuation and pay usually 1% to 3% better than the typical CD along with the tax-deferred benefits.

Many investors do not realize the tremendous benefit that an AAA-rated annuity might offer. Not only do all your earnings grow tax deferred, you earn superior rates as well. Perhaps the biggest advantage is, if the account is set up correctly, it can be a protected asset if you ever have to claim Medicaid. This means Medicaid cannot take your money. Certain provisions and caveats exist, so be sure to get sound, professional advice. Not only do you also receive the interest tax deferred, but it is not included when you compute your gross income for the taxability of Social Security benefits. This is significant now that up to 85% of your benefits may be vulnerable to taxation.

Although not typically defined as safe money, many people invest in mutual funds, a tactic I usually encourage. However, most investors buy and sell and then pay taxes on the capital gains. This can all be avoided by purchasing a variable annuity.

THE ADVANTAGES INCLUDE:

- No matter how often you buy or sell mutual funds, as long as the assets stay inside the annuity you are not required to pay capital gains tax.

- You can choose your favorite mutual funds (whether or not they have a load) since inside the annuity the funds have no front-end load. All of your money works for you.

- If, for example, you invest in an annuity that has 20TH CENTURY, FIDELITY, and OPPENHEIMER, you can switch as often as you wish from family to family to any fund offered, without penalty or fees.

- There is an insurance benefit – if you die and the value of your fund is less than your contribution, your heirs are guaranteed the amount you originally invested.

OTHER CD ALTERNATIVES

Why do people insist on investing in CDs from local banks and accept low interest rates when they can go directly to the largest banks in the country and receive higher yields? You still get access to your funds and toll-free phone numbers to call. You don't have to accept the lower yields offered by local financial institutions!

As opposed to CDs, many large, very secure companies are offering bonds and secured notes paying very handsome interest rates. I have seen five-year bonds earning as much as 8%. Of course, your principal will not be insured by the FDIC.

Regardless of what you do, be careful of *Long-Term Bonds* and *Bond Funds*. Even a government bond fund can lose money when interest rates rise. Most bond funds have maturities averaging over 20 years. *A good rule of thumb is – for every 1% rise in interest rates, your share value will decrease 10%. So, be wary of the high yielding funds, and go for a shorter term maturity.*

All investments contain risks, fees and expenses. Never invest before reading the prospectus material and thoroughly understanding your investments.

PART TWO

ESTATE PLANNING

CHAPTER 8

The Estate Plan:
Wealth Transfer

If you plan wisely before retirement, you should have accomplished your first goal by the time you retire which is accumulating enough assets to live comfortably for the remainder of your life. Sometimes unfortunate circumstances can take away the assets you worked so hard to create. Probate costs and estate fees can take a tremendous toll on an estate. If your estate is structured incorrectly, or you use poor financial planning, you can lose the assets you worked so hard to accumulate through your lifetime.

What happens after your death? If you want to keep control before *and* after death, pay the least amount of taxes and have the greatest ease changing of ownership, *have a plan!*

WHAT SENIORS STRIVE TO ACCOMPLISH WITH A GOOD ESTATE PLAN:

1. In the event of an illness, someone like a spouse, relative or friend should have access to your funds to pay your bills and make medical decisions in your behalf. Most people suffer from serious illness before dying, yet most people hold their assets in very detrimental ways. Many times property and assets are unavailable for your own maintenance or accessible to a loved one.

2. While you are physically and mentally healthy, you should express your preference in writing regarding maintenance on life support systems should they be implemented only for the purpose of prolonging your inevitable death.

3. You want your assets to pass to loved ones with the least delay, outside intervention, costs and fees in the event of your untimely death.

4. You want your beneficiaries to pay as few taxes as possible.

5. You want to be absolutely certain that assets pass directly and unquestionably to your beneficiaries. Frequently, problems arise because of your previous spouses or your children's spouses. These days many families are composed of multiple marriages and multiple sets of children and grandchildren.

6. You want your assets protected so you do not have to spend all your savings on nursing home care before Medicaid steps in with financial assistance.

PROBATE

An important ingredient in creating a good estate plan is the reduction of an estate's exposure to *Probate.* Probate is the legal method of transferring title of property from one person to another when the title holder is deceased. A probate can also occur if a person survives an accident or illness which leaves him or her incompetent or disabled. This action is known as conservatorship. All titled property will qualify for probate, including stocks, CDs, savings accounts, real estate, automobiles and personal property.

When an estate goes through the probate process, the court will make sure that all the debts are paid and that the property is distributed according to the directions in your will. Probate does not happen automatically – usually the Executor of the will begins the probate process. As much as you may want to avoid probate, as a beneficiary the assets will be unavailable to you until probate is satisfied and the judge frees the funds.

Although many probate avoidance techniques are utilized, most estates still end up going through probate – if not on the death of the first spouse, then upon the death of the second spouse. Although state laws differ, it is possible that by simply owning one home you could be subject to probate (check your state for specific minimum probate regulations).

THERE ARE MANY EXPENSES AND PROBLEMS ASSOCIATED WITH PROBATE SUCH AS:

1. It is lengthy – averaging over two years.

2. It is impersonal. Any stranger can learn your family affairs.

3. Probate is very costly. The probate fees are set by statute, and are non-negotiable. Also, probate fees are figured on the gross value of your estate. In other words if you have a $200,000 house with a $180,000 mortgage, the estate is computed on the $200,000 figure. Fees can run 6% to 8% of the gross value.

4. By going through the probate process you lose control over the assets and probate is contestable. That means anyone who disagrees with your will can contest its contents. The obvious result is the very real possibility that your estate will not be disbursed exactly as you wished it to be.

WEALTH TRANSFER TECHNIQUES
PROTECTING ASSETS AND AVOIDING PROBATE

USING A WILL

The most simple definition of a *Will* is that it is a letter directed the judge of a probate court to oversee the disposition of your estate and carry out your wishes as you have outlined them.

Since this matter is confusing and unpleasant it does not get discussed. Many myths on the subject arise as people try to convince themselves that they will not have to go through probate and they try to forget about the subject.

Always remember *where there is a will there is a probate. No matter how carefully a will is drafted it will go through probate. Below is a chart showing the process.*

Even small estates go through probate. Many times you will go through probate with a little as owning one house, or a total estate value of $60,000.

As a result of probate costs and fees, time delays, emotional trauma, and the chance that your assets will not go to your children, a will is usually not the best estate planning tool. However, if you don't mind the court's intervention and want a judge to oversee your affairs, a will might be the best alternative.

Another option is to plan nothing. Doing nothing is similar as having a will in the fact that your estate will go through probate. The only difference is that the judge has no idea how you wanted funds to be distributed and who you wanted to distribute them (Executor/ Executrix). In that case the judge will select your next of kin. This plan ensures you total loss of control and will result in high fees and costs to your estate.

YOUR ESTATE EXECUTOR'S DUTIES
Assuming you died testate with a legal will

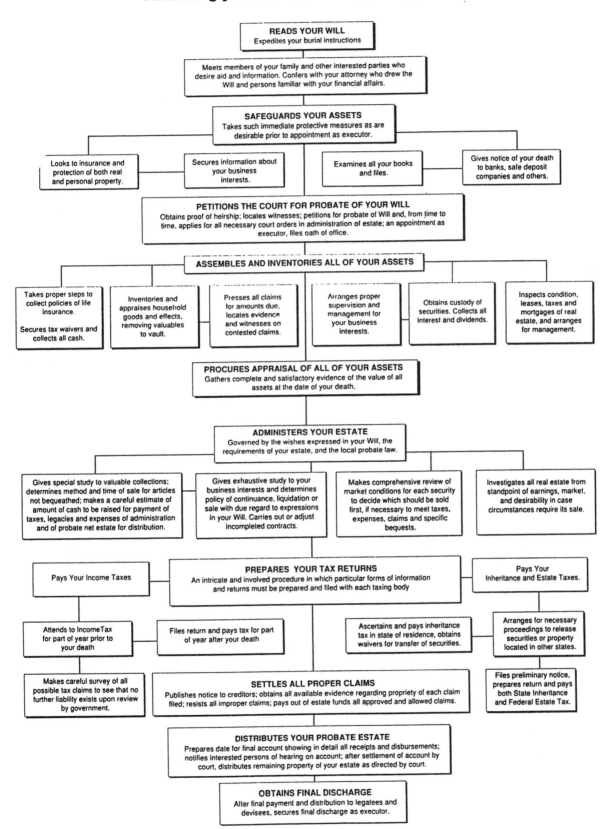

READS YOUR WILL
Expedites your burial instructions

Meets members of your family and other interested parties who desire aid and information. Confers with your attorney who drew the Will and persons familiar with your financial affairs.

SAFEGUARDS YOUR ASSETS
Takes such immediate protective measures as are desirable prior to appointment as executor.

Looks to insurance and protection of both real and personal property.

Secures information about your business interests.

Examines all your books and files.

Gives notice of your death to banks, safe deposit companies and others.

PETITIONS THE COURT FOR PROBATE OF YOUR WILL
Obtains proof of heirship; locates witnesses; petitions for probate of Will and, from time to time, applies for all necessary court orders in administration of estate; an appointment as executor, files oath of office.

ASSEMBLES AND INVENTORIES ALL OF YOUR ASSETS

Takes proper steps to collect policies of life insurance.
Secures tax waivers and collects all cash.

Inventories and appraises household goods and effects, removing valuables to vault.

Presses all claims for amounts due, locates evidence and witnesses on contested claims.

Arranges proper supervision and management for your business interests.

Obtains custody of securities. Collects all interest and dividends.

Inspects condition, leases, taxes and mortgages of real estate, and arranges for management.

PROCURES APPRAISAL OF ALL OF YOUR ASSETS
Gathers complete and satisfactory evidence of the value of all assets at the date of your death.

ADMINISTERS YOUR ESTATE
Governed by the wishes expressed in your Will, the requirements of your estate, and the local probate law.

Gives special study to valuable collections; determines method and time of sale for articles not bequeathed; makes a careful estimate of amount of cash to be raised for payment of taxes, legacies and expenses of administration and of probate net estate for distribution.

Gives exhaustive study to your business interests and determines policy of continuance, liquidation or sale with due regard to expressions in your Will. Carries out or adjust incompleted contracts.

Makes comprehensive review of market conditions for each security to decide which should be sold first, if necessary to meet taxes, expenses, claims and specific bequests.

Investigates all real estate from standpoint of earnings, market, and desirability in case circumstances require its sale.

Pays Your Income Taxes

PREPARES YOUR TAX RETURNS
An intricate and involved procedure in which particular forms of information and returns must be prepared and filed with each taxing body

Pays Your Inheritance and Estate Taxes.

Attends to Income Tax for part of year prior to your death

Files return and pays tax for part of year after your death

Ascertains and pays inheritance tax in state of residence, obtains waivers for transfer of securities.

Arranges for necessary proceedings to release securities or property located in other states.

Makes careful survey of all possible tax claims to see that no further liability exists upon review by government.

SETTLES ALL PROPER CLAIMS
Publishes notice to creditors; obtains all available evidence regarding propriety of each claim filed; resists all improper claims; pays out of estate funds all approved and allowed claims.

Files preliminary notice, prepares return and pays both State Inheritance and Federal Estate Tax.

DISTRIBUTES YOUR PROBATE ESTATE
Prepares date for final account showing in detail all receipts and disbursements; notifies interested persons of hearing on account; after settlement of account by court, distributes remaining property of your estate as directed by court.

OBTAINS FINAL DISCHARGE
After final payment and distribution to legatees and devisees, secures final discharge as executor.

JOINT TENANCY

Joint Tenancy (**JT**) is a very common and popular form of titling assets. One reason people utilize joint tenancy is because it will avoid probate. Although common, it is *often a poor way to title assets.* Problems with joint tenancy are numerous and dangerous. When you buy a house, open a savings account or make an investment and you are asked how you want to hold title, think twice before placing the property or investments in joint tenancy. Joint tenancy is one of the worst ways of holding title for several reasons.

If a husband and a wife own something together (house or brokerage account), they will usually own it as joint tenants. But what happens if one of the spouses becomes ill? What if it is a prolonged or serious sickness resulting in that spouse's incapacitation? The other spouse cannot sell the house or refinance it because this requires both signatures. You can see the potential problems if you need money out of the equity and you wish to refinance, or simply move to a smaller home. *Without both signatures, you can do nothing.*

The only way to get access without both signatures is to go to court and go through the same things as you would for probate. In fact, the procedure is a living probate called *Conservatorship.* A conservatorship action can be just as long and costly as going through probate.

A good document to have in your estate plan is a

DURABLE POWER OF ATTORNEY FOR PROPERTY.

**This would help obtain access to a piece of real estate
if the owner becomes incapacitated.**

The second problem is loss of control. *Be very careful before adding children as joint tenants with you on your assets.* Although you may be doing this with the best of intentions, the repercussions could be disastrous. The following are just a few:

Should your child be sued or file for bankruptcy, you could lose your assets. Or if you live in a community property state and your child gets a divorce, his or her spouse may have a legal interest in your property. Or your child may think of you as incompetent and try to control your assets.

If you gift an asset over $10,000 to someone this could be considered a taxable gift. And adding someone on an account with you could be considered gifting. You may be able to avoid immediate tax using your once in a lifetime $600,000 exclusion but this will reduce the amount that you will be allowed to use after your death. Giving a gift while you are living instead of after you die may result in much higher capital gains taxes and you will lose your step-up in cost basis for tax purposes.

You have lost control because every person you put on title with you now has to approve anything you might do with the property (refinance, sell or borrow).

A final problem with owning property in joint tenancy deals with taxes and the cost basis of the property. Cost basis is defined as the original cost of the property. The difference between the current market value and the cost basis is called the taxable gain. When a person dies, his or her property will receive a *Step-Up In Tax Basis* (IRS Code 1014b). This means your cost basis will be increased and will incur less taxes. However, the amount of the step-up in basis for tax purposes depends on how you hold title to the property.

Consider the following example: A married couple purchased a home for $50,000. The house is now worth $150,000. Assume the husband dies. Half of the property will enjoy a step-up in basis to the fair market value of $75,000. Now assume that the surviving spouse sells the property for $150,000. She has a $50,000 taxable gain because *her half of the property did not step-up in basis.*

Now assume the house was held under different title, such as community property in a living trust. The whole property enjoys a step-up in basis, resulting in no taxable gain when the survivor either sells the house for $150,000 or when the survivor dies and the house gets sold.

You must research your state laws before executing this technique since different states have different criteria. However, my point is you should research what is best for your situation. However, in most circumstances, holding property as joint tenants is very detrimental.

STEP-UP IN BASIS

JOINT TENANCY VS. LIVING TRUSTS

Basis is the original cost of the property involved. The difference between the current market value and the basis is a taxable gain. IRS Code 1014 (b) permits a step-up in basis (increase) when a person dies. How much of a step-up depends on how that person held title.

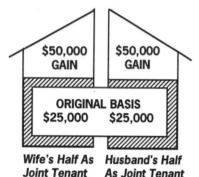

AS JOINT TENANTS, A MARRIED COUPLE PURCHASED THEIR HOME IN 1969 FOR $50,000. THE CURRENT VALUE IS $150,000.

AFTER THE DEATH OF A SPOUSE

IF THE HOUSE IS OWNED AS JOINT TENANTS:

NEW BASIS $100,000

IF THE HOUSE PUT INTO A LIVING TRUST:

NEW BASIS $150,000

THE DIFFERENCE TO SURVIVING SPOUSE

JOINT TENANCY		TRUST
$150,000	MARKET VALUE	$150,000
$100,000	LESS BASIS	$150,000
$50,000	TAXABLE GAIN	$0
$10,000	CAPITAL GAINS ESTIMATED TAX	$0

TRUSTS

One sensible technique used to transfer assets to avoid probate is utilizing various types of trusts and is outlined in the next chapter.

CHAPTER 9

Creating and Utilizing
a Trust

A very good option for wealth transfer is the creation of a *Trust.* Trusts allow you to avoid probate and many other problems associated with transfers of assets.

In the broad context there are two major types: *Testamentary Trusts* and *Living Trusts.* The difference is that a testamentary trust becomes effective upon death, and is created as a result of a will. If you created a will and upon your death you wanted your assets to be held in trust for an heir, that would be a testamentary trust. A living trust becomes effective immediately once the trust is created and finalized. Many times the trust will continue to last after your death. The living trust is an effective tool to use for estate planning purposes. Although it is not a cure-all for all your problems, a living trust has many advantages.

A living trust is a legal document that handles your estate differently than a will. There is no probate with assets held in a living trust. As a result you will eliminate the court costs, time delays, and loss of privacy. As previously discussed, a will is very easy to argue or contest, but trusts are very difficult to argue against.

Think of a living trust as a private corporation that you implement. You don't have to register it anywhere, you don't need a separate tax identification number (although sometimes appropriate) or any other mythical obligations. When you create this "private corporation" you automatically become the creator *(Settler* or *Trustor* in legal terms). Usually you nominate yourself as the trustee or both you and your spouse as co-trustees which is equivalent to being the president. You set forth all the provisions you wish to have, such as placing no restrictions on what you do with the assets during your lifetime. You now nominate who you want to be president if you were to die, or become incapacitated, and this new president is called the *Successor Trustee.*

Through the trust you designate to the successor trustee exactly how you want the assets handled in the event of your death, exactly whom you wish to have the assets, when they can have them and under what conditions. Since you are the president, you can change direction as often as you want with absolutely no problem. In fact, most of the changes are anticipated and you can do them yourself.

If you create a trust you must place all the assets into the name of the trust, taking them out of an individual or joint tenancy title, and transfer them into the name of the trust. Technically, as an individual (or married couple) you own nothing, your trust owns everything. If you own nothing, you have no probate.

ADVANTAGES OF A TRUST

Most people have neither heard of a trust nor have they felt they needed one. However, if for no other reason than avoiding probate, a trust benefits many people and should be considered more often.

AVOIDANCE OF PROBATE

Properly structured, the assets in a living trust will avoid probate. One of the first objectives in a good estate plan is to keep control and preserve your estate. Since probate throws the estate into the courts, you lose control. As a result of the high costs, you do not preserve your estate either.

THE DIFFERENCE BETWEEN
PROBATE AND A LIVING TRUST

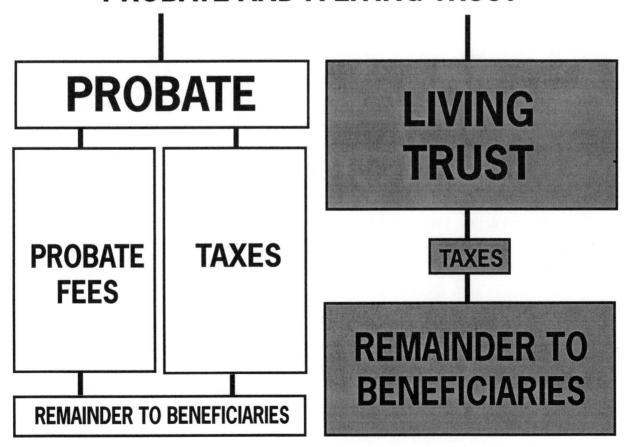

PROBATE

PROBATE FEES	TAXES

REMAINDER TO BENEFICIARIES

LIVING TRUST

TAXES

REMAINDER TO BENEFICIARIES

The trust does not magically protect your assets, however. Think of it logically – a living trust is similar to a private corporation. Corporations never get sick and never die, only people do. The probate court only comes into being when someone dies. When you set up a trust, and nominate yourself trustee and subsequently die, the trust doesn't die, and you have already nominated a new successor trustee.

CONTROL

Nowadays, especially with so many divorces, second marriages, stepchildren and divorced children, any time an estate becomes public and goes to probate, the estate becomes vulnerable to argument and may be contested. Since the trust is a private document, it is virtually incontestable.

In addition, while living, you carry on your business as normal. You can open or close bank accounts, buy and sell real estate and stocks -- whatever you want. As long as you purchase these assets in the name of your trust, everything will be fine. You do not have to change the trust. I do encourage you to keep a *Document Locator* in order to make it easy for your heirs to locate your assets.

Another advantage to keeping control is that you can be absolutely sure who is going to receive your inheritance. Say you had a will and wanted to leave your daughter money, but unfortunately your daughter died. You might want the inheritance to go to your grandchild but who do you think will get the money? Chances are your daughter's husband will manage the money for your grandchild. If you do not trust your son-in-law or do not want him to have this responsibility, your wishes would count for very little.

If, however, you had a living trust, you would make provisions to state something to the effect that in the event your daughter dies, you want the money to go to your grandchild at the age of 25. (Most wills designate age 18; with a trust you can extend the age). Furthermore, you would want the trustee to manage the money instead of your daughter's husband. The trustee will probably be your other son, daughter, or professional trust institution.

A TRUST HELPS REDUCE ESTATE TAXES

As we have discussed in great detail, estate taxes could be the largest tax burden your family will ever pay. The tax rate is between 37% and 55%. If, after the second death, your estate is worth $1,000,000, the estate tax would be over $200,000. This is neither negotiable nor does it go unclaimed. In fact, the IRS demands this money within nine months after your death. How many of your children can write a check for $200,000? Chances are they will have to sell your property at "fire sale" prices to come up with the money to pay the taxes.

GIFT AND ESTATE TAXES
(UNIFIED TRANSFER TAX)

Amount Subject to Tax			
(A) Exceeding	But not Exceeding	Tax on Amount in Column A	Tax Rate (%) on Excess Over Amount in Column A
$ 0	$ 10,000	$ 0	18
10,000	20,000	1,800	20
20,000	40,000	3,800	22
40,000	60,000	8,200	24
60,000	80,000	13,000	26
80,000	100,000	18,200	28
100,000	150,000	23,800	30
150,000	250,000	38,800	32
250,000	500,000	70,800	34
500,000	750,000	155,800	37
750,000	1,000,000	248,300	39
1,000,000	1,250,000	345,800	41
1,250,000	1,500,000	448,300	43
1,500,000	2,000,000	555,800	45
2,000,000	2,500,000	780,800	49
2,500,000	3,000,000	1,025,800	53
3,000,000	10,000,000	1,290,800	55
10,000,000	21,040,000	5,140,800	60
21,040,000		11,764,800	55

When creating a trust, you could put an *A/B Provision* on the trust. Technically you will be creating two trusts; an *Exemption Trust* and a *Survivor Trust.* I remember it easier as the "A" trust being the above ground trust, the "B" being the below-ground trust.

Most couples use what is called a *Marital Deduction.* This means when one spouse passes away they gift all of their property to the surviving spouse, *free of taxes.* Marital deduction is a nice benefit but you just wasted a $600,000 exemption to which the deceased spouse was entitled to give. If both spouses fully utilize the exemption you can receive a total benefit equal to $1,200,000. This is obtained by creating your living trust with a provision that automatically separates the trust upon the death of the first spouse, thus the A/B provision. Each trust will now be able to claim its own $600,000 exemption.

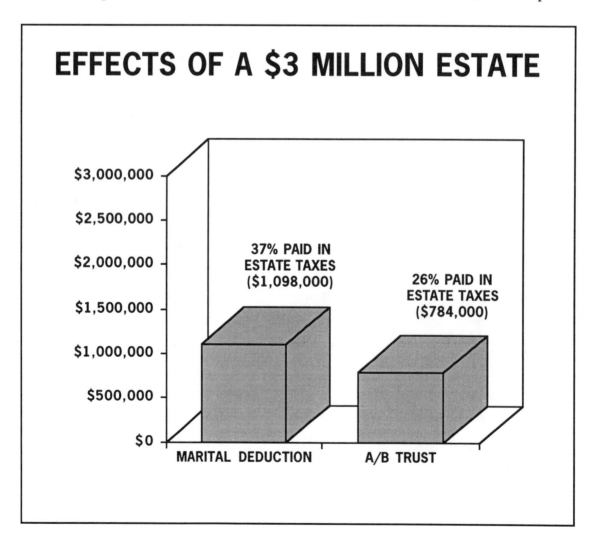

EFFECTS OF A $3 MILLION ESTATE

- $3,000,000
- $2,500,000
- $2,000,000
- $1,500,000
- $1,000,000
- $500,000
- $0

37% PAID IN ESTATE TAXES ($1,098,000)

26% PAID IN ESTATE TAXES ($784,000)

MARITAL DEDUCTION   A/B TRUST

HERE`S HOW MUCH IT WILL COST A $3 MILLION ESTATE TO PAY ESTATE TAXES, DEPENDING ON THE TAX PLANNING OPTION USED

1. Using the Marital Deduction, no estate taxes are due when the first spouse dies; but when the second spouse dies, $1,098,000, or 37% of the estate, would be consumed by estate taxes.

2. An A/B living trust protects $1.2 million, but that still leaves $784,000 in estate taxes, or 26% of the estate.

Everyone is allowed a one-time exclusion of $600,000 on the estate before the estate taxes are levied. As long as your estate is under $600,000, you don't have to pay estate taxes.

There is a bill currently in Congress trying to reduce this amount to $200,000 per spouse. If you are married, usually the assets are co-mingled and allows only one gift for the both of you of $600,000. However, by separating the two trusts, you each will receive a $600,000 exclusion, allowing the estate to be as large as $1,200,000 before the taxes are levied.

For couples who have children from previous marriages, creating an A/B trust can help solve other problems. Once the A/B trust is established, neither spouse can change the other's beneficiaries once that spouse has passed away. This means if the husband or wife has remarried, they cannot change the deceased spouse's beneficiaries to include the new husband, or to give the money to his children.

A TRUST PREVENTS CONSERVATORSHIP

As mentioned previously, joint tenancy can be a terrible way to hold title. One of the worst problems is the fact that if one spouse becomes sick or incapacitated, the other joint tenant will lose all control. That tenant cannot sell or refinance the property. The healthy spouse would have to go through conservatorship action which is another court proceeding that is almost as long and as costly as probate.

For example, if your husband had a stroke, and you need to sell your house to buy a smaller house, you will be unable to sell if he cannot sign the documents.

The living trust, properly implemented, has provisions stating that if one spouse gets sick the other can make medical decisions, sell your house or refinance it.

THE TRUST IS COMPLETELY REVOCABLE

A revocable living trust can be established, changed, or canceled at any time, so long as both trustors or creators of the trust are living.

IMPORTANT QUESTIONS TO ASK AND PROVISIONS TO INCLUDE WHEN ESTABLISHING YOUR TRUST

When a client establishes a trust he or she should ask the advisor what the total fee will be, including all the necessary documents, the funding of the trust, quitclaiming the properties and notarization. If the estate is over $600,000, it is going to be an A/B trust.

You want to know if you will be receiving the A/B trust. You should be sure that you have full and complete control over the assets while both of you are living. After the first spouse's death, you will not be able to change beneficiaries. This is partly what the A/B trust would accomplish. The other task it will accomplish is to protect your estate from estate taxes up to $1,200,000 (under current law).

Remember, this is your trust that you are creating. Put the provisions in that you choose. If you feel that you might have a child who is incompetent, give the discretion to the trustee that the child must receive funds. You have the prerogative of giving your trustee a great deal of control or very little control. You might say, "Upon my death, sell all assets immediately and distribute equally to my children."

You should ask what will happen to the assets after both spouses die, and how they will be disbursed to the beneficiaries. Obviously, through a properly structured trust, the trustee would be in charge of that process.

WHAT HAPPENS IF A SPOUSE GETS SICK

As you may know most people have an illness before passing away. This is a hardship especially for single individuals, widow and widowers. What if you have an illness – what happens to your affairs if you cannot make decisions? Usually the courts will decide who will make medical decisions and who can have access to your bank accounts – a procedure that is alarming to me. *You should decide who can have access to your finances.* A properly structured trust would address such an issue.

In addition to the trust, the durable power of attorney and living will accomplishes these tasks.

WHO SHOULD MY TRUSTEES BE?

The trustee should be someone in whom you have confidence and faith. Although the trustee is required to follow certain laws, codes and ethics, trustees are not strictly governed. The trustee should be honest, good with financial matters, and someone that will represent you and your wishes accurately. Ideally the trustee would be the creator of the trust.

After your death and your spouse's death, if applicable, consider using one of the beneficiaries as acting trustee. If the beneficiaries are not competent to manage the affairs, you can hire another relative or friend, or even an institutional or corporate trustee. There are companies that are in business to act as trustees. One possible solution is to have a joint trustee – one being a beneficiary, and one being an institutional trustee. If there have been previous marriages and children, possibly one child from each side of the family should represent as trustee. As you all know, money can turn friends into enemies, so try not to select more then two trustees.

First you must ask yourself who would you like to have as your trustee. Usually it would be you and your spouse, or just you alone. But after you are gone, or if you get sick, who can carry out your wishes? You can pick as many trustees as you like but one or two with an alternate is the best choice.

CHOOSING BENEFICIARIES

Make sure that your gift is directed to a specific person – for instance, your son John, not John's family. That way it is not *Family Property.* Technically, an inheritance is to be kept separate property by the recipient. If your beneficiary keeps the inheritance separate property, chances are if the beneficiary divorces, the funds will maintain their separateness.

TRANSFER OF PROPERTY

Until the property is placed into the name of the trust, the trust is like a vase without water. You must change all of your assets into the name of the trust, so each one of your statements, deeds, and bank accounts reads your name as trustee for your trust. You must make copies of your trust (or the first page and the signature page), send them to the various places where you hold assets, and make sure they transfer the name into your trust, exactly as it is shown.

WHAT OTHER DOCUMENTS SHOULD BE INCLUDED IN AN ESTATE PLAN?

POUROVER WILL

This document is your last will and testament. The difference of the *Pourover Provision* states that you give everything to your trust. Look at the pourover will as your safety net. Once you create your trust it is your job to remember to always put your assets in the name of the trust. If your assets are not in the trust, they will be part of your estate and will go through probate. *Remember, a pourover will won't help you avoid probate, it simply gives instructions to the judge to place your assets into trust.*

DURABLE POWER OF ATTORNEY

A Durable Power of Attorney is a useful and important document. Many powers of attorney become nullified upon a person's incapacitation, whereas a durable power of attorney remains in effect even after a person's incapacitation.

A DPA For Property and Financial Issues will allow the person you appoint as *Attorney-In-Fact* to carry on with important property and financial decisions such as buying and selling assets or paying creditors.

A DPA For Health Purposes will give power to the person you appoint to make medical decision on your behalf. This might include operating decisions, certain medical treatments or autopsy. You should appoint someone whom you know well and whom you feel will responsibly perform these tasks. Obviously this is preferable to a state-appointed administrator.

LIVING WILL

A living will is a critical estate planning document for those individuals who do not wish to be connected to life support systems in the event of a terminal illness or accident. The document certifies that at the time of signing you are competent and understand your decision.

Usually a living will states that if two physicians certify you are terminally ill and life support will only prolong an inevitable death within a short period of time, it should not be used. I would recommend having a professional create this document, getting it witnessed, and then making copies to be kept by someone in your home, in your safe deposit box and in your medical file.

Note that some living wills are incorporated into a durable power of attorney for health care. If this practice is legal in your state, then it might work. However, usually I would recommend keeping these two documents separate.

ANATOMICAL GIFT DECLARATION

If you wish to be an organ donor, this is included in your gift declaration.

DOCUMENT LOCATOR

Although *not used enough,* it is this document that will organize your estate and help your beneficiaries account for all of your assets. It lists your assets, who holds title to them (the trust), where they are located, property deeds, the location of safe deposit keys, passbook saving accounts and insurance policies. You would be surprised how many millions of dollars are never claimed from banks and insurance companies every year because the heirs are not aware of the existence of assets.

HOW OFTEN SHOULD YOUR ESTATE PLAN BE REVIEWED OR CHANGED?

The estate plan should be changed only if you have material changes such as a change of beneficiary or change of trustee. Also, the estate plan should be amended if the laws and regulations change that affect the estate plan.

The plan should be reviewed at least once a year. You should make sure everything is as you wish it to be. Sometimes children grow older and become better equipped to handle financial responsibilities that you would have not entrusted to them at an earlier age.

Remember, you do not need to change your estate plan documents every time you buy or sell assets. Most living trusts allocate assets using percentages, never stating specific assets. As long as you remember to always buy assets in the name of the trust, that is sufficient. It is recommended that you track all your assets using a document locator.

COMMON PROVISIONS TO INCLUDE IN YOUR LIVING TRUST OR ESTATE PLAN

A TRUST IS A PRIVATE DOCUMENT THAT YOU CREATE. CERTAIN PROVISIONS THAT SHOULD BE INCLUDED ARE:

1. Make that sure you stipulate that children and grandchildren do not receive assets until the age of 25. Perhaps something like, "assets will be held in trust until my grandchild reaches the age of 25 with the exception of education, medical and living expenses."

2. Specifically name your beneficiaries. Don't give a gift to your daughter's family but name your daughter specifically. Also encourage her to hold these assets as separate property once she receives them in case of a divorce.

3. Allow for certain provisions that make the beneficiaries irrevocable after the first death. This will prevent your spouse from remarrying and changing the beneficiary to the new spouse.

4. If your child dies, specify if the beneficiary is your grandchild or if you prefer it to be another one of your children.

> **5. Also specify if you DO NOT WANT someone to get something. This way a judge will know that you INTENDED to keep someone from getting your assets.**

WHO NEEDS A TRUST?

The living trust part of an estate plan is no longer just for the wealthy. In many states if you own a home and have assets over $60,000, your estate will be probated. Anyone who wants a private process, who has loyal successor trustees, and who wants to avoid probate should learn more about trusts.

HOW ARE CHANGES MADE TO A TRUST?

Obviously there are many types of trusts, different trusts will be discussed under the advanced planning techniques. However, if we are discussing revocable living trusts as we have been, the trust is completely revocable and can be changed at any time. In fact, if you do not need the trust or do not wish to have it at a certain point, transfer assets back into your own name and then tear up the trust. If you want to make a change, all it takes is a simple amendment.

USE PERCENTAGES

In disbursing the assets in a trust you usually gift assets in percentages instead of dollar amounts, actual accounts or pieces of real estate. That way, if you sell an asset before your death, less confusion arises. If your trust says that you want your two children to split your estate 50%/50%, it is much easier for all concerned.

WHAT OBLIGATIONS DOES THE SURVIVING SPOUSE HAVE AFTER THE DEATH OF THEIR SPOUSE IN A TRUST?

This subject should be seriously considered and extensively reviewed while both spouses are living and healthy. If you have a revocable living trust (with an A/B provision), the survivor will have the responsibility of becoming sole trustee. If you are misinformed, you may be in for more problems than you anticipate.

After the first death, there is a great deal of administrative work. You have to keep accurate records about the assets, cash flow, acquisitions and sales. Assets may continually have to be appraised as well. After the first death, extra tax forms may be required for the trust.

You must complete a final tax form for the deceased. In addition, you will usually complete a tax return for the "B" trust every year as well.

If a spouse dies in an A/B trust it is wise to appraise all assets and create two logs: one for the "A" trust and one for the "B" trust. List the principal assets in each trust and the income received from each asset. If you sell an asset, log it in as a sale and when you make a purchase, log it in as a purchase.

Upon the first death in an A/B trust, usually you will split assets equally in terms of dollar amounts, up to $600,000 for the "B" trust. However, be sure you place the assets in the correct trusts. Some assets are better in the "A" trust rather than the "B" trust.

For example, your home might be better to remain in the "A" trust because you might want to sell it at a later date. When you sell it, you might take advantage of Section 121 of the tax code in order to reduce any capital gain exposure up to $125,000. If the asset were in the "B" trust, since it is now another entity and not in an individual's name or a revocable living trust, you cannot take advantage of a Section 121 since it is only offered to individuals.

Most often the services of an experienced estate planning accountant must be retained. But all of this work is far simpler than the probate process in many states. However, you should plan in advance and understand what is expected of the trustee after your death. One major negative aspect may be the strain it puts on the relationship of the trustee and the beneficiaries. This may put the trustee in a precarious position. If the estate would have gone through probate, you might be able to blame your problem on the judicial system. This is not true with a trust. This is the reason some people opt for an institutional trustee, such as a trust department at a bank.

CHAPTER 10

Advanced
Property Considerations

Advanced estate planning techniques are critical because estate taxes can run as high as 55%. Loss of control of an estate is common without utilizing certain techniques. Therefore it is common sense for you to have a working knowledge of advanced estate planning. Also, you must have a working knowledge of how to protect estates from creditors and bankruptcy.

REVERSE MORTGAGES

A *Reverse Annuity Mortgage* allows you to take income out of the equity build-up in your home. A reverse mortgage is exactly what it says – the opposite of the typical home mortgage. Instead of borrowing a lump sum that must be repaid in monthly (or bi-monthly) installments, you can receive monthly payments or a lump sum of cash in an amount based on your age and the value of your home. The loan balance that you have received, plus interest, does not have to be repaid until you die, sell your home, or move.

You must be at least 62 years of age to obtain a reverse mortgage. A reverse mortgage is not a mortgage in the conventional sense. You can't obtain a reverse mortgage until your original mortgage is paid off (or unless you paid cash for your home). Suppose you own your home and you need more income. The older you are at the time of taking a reverse mortgage the more income you will probably receive.

Reverse mortgage loan advances are non-taxable. Furthermore, they are not added into your total gross income for Social Security or Medicare benefits.

The kinds of plans are as many as the types of mortgages – fixed, variable, and others.

Like any mortgage, a nice protection feature is the Federal Truth In Lending Act, which requires lenders to inform you about the plan's terms and costs. Be sure you are very clear about them before signing. The lenders also must disclose the *Annual Percentage Rate (APR)* and payment terms. Lenders must provide specific information about the variable rate feature on plans with adjustable rates. In plans with credit lines, lenders also must inform you of any charges to open and use the account, such as appraisals, credit reports, escrow or attorney fees, and title insurance.

There are some disadvantages to this strategy, however. The interest rates sound very attractive and rightfully so. They might as well quote 10% or 12% interest on the income you will be receiving, because they get to keep the equity left in the house.

Although the interest is alluring, I usually want to keep my principal in the house. If you need money, you could consider a *Home Equity Loan* or taking a small first mortgage. Perhaps if you had no beneficiaries or charities and wanted the highest possible interest, this would make sense, but first carefully review all your options.

Some people just sell the house, move into something less expensive, pay cash for it, and use the extra funds for their needs.

HOMESTEADING

Regardless of whether your home is held in joint tenancy, in a living trust, or as a sole individual, many people still choose to *Homestead* their home. Of course, there are many requirements and you must live in a state that allows homesteading. If you do, a homestead will allow a certain amount of protection from creditors on the equity in your home.

Note: Homesteading is not a difficult process and could save your equity from various creditors. You should research this subject further and examine your state's laws to determine if it makes sense for you.

The Homestead Allowance was designed to preserve the residence for the benefit of the surviving spouse and a decedent's minor children in case that the owner of a residence should die with a substantial amount of debt, or in the case of a lawsuit.

Some states defined the residence for qualifying for property by the number of acres (to include adjacent land). The acreage could be as little as half an acre to 40 acres. Some states define the amount in terms of dollars (for example, $50,000 is protected).

AVOIDING CAPITAL GAINS

It's the old "good news–bad news" story. The good news is you did well, the asset appreciated and now it's time to take your profits. The bad news is you have to pay *Capital Gains.* Depending on your tax bracket, the capital gain can be well over 30% (*after* state and federal taxes). Obviously that decreases the return on your savvy investment by a healthy margin. Some wise investors use the Section 121 exclusion.

SECTION 121

People who are 55 years or older who have a capital gain on a home can sell the house and use Section 121 to eliminate $125,000 of a capital gain. So, if you have $125,000 worth of a capital gain and you elect the Section 121, you will not owe estate taxes. Rules do exist – you can only use the exclusion once. Even if you are on a second marriage and one spouse previously used a Section 121, the new married couple cannot use it. And you must have resided in your residence for three out of five years (not necessarily consecutively).

GIFT-APPRECIATED ASSETS

If you own a stock or real estate for which you paid $10 and it is now worth $100, instead of selling the stock and making a gift of the cash, instead gift the stock. As long as your gift is under $10,000 you will not have estate tax or capital gain on the gift. *The catch is, whenever a gift is made while the person making the gift is living, the recipient will owe the capital gains when they sell the gift, based on the original basis value.* In this case, $10. If the person making the gift held it and made it a part of the estate or held the assets in community property (preferably in the name of a trust), then the basis for tax purposes would be whatever the value is upon death. Therefore, in this case, the basis would be $100. If the stock was immediately sold, the $100 would be *not* be taxed.

BUY A BIGGER HOME

No one says you cannot sell the old house and buy a bigger one. Although most people usually sell and move smaller, you can move up.

THE $600,000 ESTATE TAX EXCLUSION

If you are confident that your assets are not going to exceed the $600,000 estate tax exclusion limit and you want to make a major gift, you might want to use the one-time $600,000 exemption (or part of it) while you're alive. However, if your estate exceeds $600,000 then the estate taxes will be excessive upon your death.

If you are married and can create a revocable living trust, and transfer your assets into the trust – that might be the answer. By creating and transferring your assets to an A/B trust, you can each maintain your own $600,000 exemption, thereby allowing an estate valued at over $1,200,000 before having to pay estate taxes.

Congress has been pressing hard to enact a new bill, to lower your estate tax exclusion limit from $600,000 to $200,000. If they succeed, more advanced strategies will be necessary on your part. That is the reason why some experts are advising large gifts now, while you are still allowed to gift up to $600,000.

CHAPTER 11

Estate Reduction Strategies

GIFTING ASSETS

The subject of *Gifting* is a complicated one and needs to be clarified. If handled correctly, gifting can help you avoid capital gains, reduce values of an estate, get funds out of an estate for Medi-Cal purposes, assist with a grandchild's education and much more. However the repercussions could be loud if you are not careful.

Anyone at any time is allowed to give a yearly gift up to $10,000 per spouse per year before a gift tax is imposed. So, if you have two children and want to give a maximum yearly gift, with two spouses you could gift a total of $40,000 per year to your two children.

The question that remains is, which asset do you gift? If you gift cash, then you do not pay taxes and the recipient of the gift does not pay a tax on the gift. Of course if the recipient invests the money, he will pay tax on any earnings. If you have an appreciated asset (stock or real estate), should you sell it and then give the gift? Think hard. If you sell it, you pay the capital gains tax. If you gift it, you avoid paying the tax. The recipient of the gift will have to pay the tax.

For example, assume you purchased stock for $5,000 and it is now worth $10,000. If you sell the stock, the capital gain will be paid by you. If you gift the stock worth $10,000, the capital gain is transferred to the recipient of the gift. The basis of the original purchase ($5,000), stays the same.

> **If you die, the entire basis of the stock (your original $5,000), is stepped-up in value to the fair market value upon your death. In this case we are assuming the fair market value is $10,000, meaning the recipient of the gift would pay no capital gains tax if the stock was sold at $10,000!**

ADVANTAGES TO GIFTING ASSETS

The point just illustrated is a big advantage. It avoids paying a capital gain on an appreciated asset. Obviously the benefactor of the gift will pay, but his tax rate could be different than yours.

If you gift assets 30 months prior to entering a nursing home, you might be eligible for Medi-Cal, provided you qualify in all other areas.

Estates over $600,000 in value will pay high estate taxes, unless further estate planning techniques are utilized.

If you gift $10,000 per year per person to keep below the $600,000 limit, it may save enormous amounts of money in estate taxes once you pass away. Unless you state that you want to use the $600,000 exclusion (or part of it), on a particular gift, while you are alive, it is reserved for use after your death. This allows you the $10,000 yearly gift per person without affecting $600,000 exemption. If you use the exemption while you are alive then you cannot use it at death.

DISADVANTAGES OF GIFTING

The biggest disadvantage is the loss of the step-up basis. If you gift assets while alive, someone will pay the capital gain tax. If it is inherited, the step-up basis will avoid the capital gain tax on most assets.

Another major problem with gifting assets is your loss of control. Many people put a son or a daughter on the title of their accounts as joint tenants. This is a form of a gift.

You lose control of your property when this is done. You cannot sell or refinance without the signatures of all parties involved. I understand you have the best of intentions, but think of the implications. What happens if the person you put on your property is sued, goes bankrupt or gets a divorce? Any of these situations can result in the loss of your property.

GENERATION SKIPPING

If you have grandchildren, a beautiful gifting technique is the *Generation Skipping Rule.* The generation skipping rule states that any gifts for health or educational purposes can be given to the grandchildren, in *unlimited amounts, free of gift taxes.* Make sure you make checks out directly to the school or health insurance carrier.

TRIM DOWN YOUR ESTATE

Although many people might disagree, think of all the assets you have in your estate that increase the value of the estate. Maybe you don't need all of them.

Remember, all of your assets over $600,000 will be taxed as high as 55%. If you are making a 10% interest rate on your investments, think of it as giving 5% to Uncle Sam. You are just acting as custodian of *his* money until you die. If you buy an ordinary life insurance policy, be sure to buy double the amount you really want, because half will go to Uncle Sam.

Think of all the life insurance you have – all the old policies, not counting the new policies that salesmen are trying to sell you. What do you need them for? If your estate is over $1,200,000, chances are after the first death, the survivor will not need a large insurance proceed. *The death benefit from a life insurance policy will increase the value of your estate.* Whenever you figure your estate's worth for estate tax purposes, remember to include the value of your life insurance. It will be included.

If you have old policies that you do not really need, cash them out, take the cash value and enjoy yourself. While you're alive, you can build the monies on the cash value or take the cash value and buy long-term care insurance. Once you pass away, Uncle Sam will thank you for his half. A very creative, sensible method of managing life insurance is covered under the Insurance Trust section.

As mentioned earlier, if your estate is growing rapidly, start slowing down, enjoy yourself and take more trips. *No matter how much planning you do, remember that "you can't take it with you."*

I know numerous people who have estates valued at over $600,000 who continue to invest in high risk investments, going for higher returns and increasing the value of the estate. My question is – would you take that kind of risk for half the return? If your aggressive mutual fund is returning 16% annually, would you take that risk for 8%? If you said "no," why not? After a certain amount, the estate taxes will be over 50% anyway. Why not take the low-risk 8%, avoid many of the headaches and don't increase your estate to the point where 50% will go to taxes? Of course, the other solution is to use the techniques and loopholes available to protect the assets and allow your estate to grow with minimal estate tax burden.

IRREVOCABLE TRUSTS

An *Irrevocable Trust* can be used to get assets out of the estate and reduce the value of the estate, and can be created in such a way to have the assets go to the heirs you have selected. Many mature Americans create an irrevocable trust and place a sum of money in the trust. The trustee might purchase a government bond, then stipulates that all income is to be received by the creators of the trust. Upon death, the trust is instructed to give the money to whomever has been previously named.

The advantage is that it reduces the size of the estate by whatever the value of the gift. The money is protected from creditors and is sure to go to your beneficiaries. All is well.

Potential disadvantages exist as well. Unlike a revocable trust, the creator cannot be the trustee or the beneficiary to have this work. You have no control or opinion. You cannot change or revoke this type of trust in any way and you might have to pay gift taxes.

In many cases the irrevocable trust will have its own income tax rate and tax ID number. This could be beneficial if, for example, you instructed the trust to retain the income it generated, and you, the creator are to get none. Now the asset is out of your estate and you are taxed on what it makes. Be careful of the amounts and potential gift tax traps or how the trust is worded. *Don't do anything until you seek professional investment assistance for your particular situation.*

IRREVOCABLE CHARITABLE REMAINDER TRUSTS

The irrevocable charitable remainder trust is one of the more popular irrevocable trusts, for many good reasons. Usually a charitable remainder trust works like this:

Assume you have a highly appreciated piece of property you no longer wish to own. Your estate is large and any possible way of reducing the amount you would pay for estate taxes would help. However, you have children whom you feel deserve what you worked so hard to earn. The property was bought many years ago for $20,000 and it is now worth $200,000. If you sold the property, the taxes would be tremendously high as a result of the capital gain. Although the property appreciates, it provides no income which is something you would like more of as your travel habits are getting more exotic.

Assume you and a qualified charity got together and drafted a charitable remainder trust. You placed the property inside the trust and immediately sell it for $200,000 once inside the trust. The trust was instructed to put the proceeds of the sale into a AAA-rated annuity that will guarantee a 9% interest rate for both you and your spouse's life.

BY SELLING THE PROPERTY <u>INSIDE</u> THE TRUST YOU ACCOMPLISHED:

1. Avoiding capital gains tax. The full $200,000 went into the annuity paying 9% instead of the net amount you would have received had you sold it and paid the taxes on your own.

2. Since, in fact, you made a charitable donation, the deductions on your taxes will be sizable.

3. Your income is now increased at over $1,500 per month.

4. Upon your death the charity will get the principal of the trust. You got the income while you were alive, but they get the asset once you die. So, you did a good deed.

Of course, the negative is that you just gave away a $200,000 asset that your beneficiaries could have used. What you should do is have the charity, inside the charitable trust, buy an insurance policy to be paid directly to your children in the amount of $200,000 after the creator(s) dies. The benefits are several. Although your estate made the gift of the property, your beneficiaries will still receive $200,000. What's more, since the irrevocable insurance trust is the owner, it is not included in the total value of your estate, so it will not be taxed or increase the size of your estate by the amount of the insurance proceeds. It bypasses your estate and goes directly to your children. Now your estate is not reduced, it did not cost you anything, you paid no taxes, in fact, you received deductions, you gave a generous donation, and all is well.

Why would the charity spend a few thousand a year on an insurance trust to pay if both trustees die? Because you gave them a $200,000 gift. It is one of the best investments they will make.

The biggest downside is that you lose control of the money. You had better be certain that this is what you want to do before doing it.

TWO COMMON TYPES OF CHARITABLE TRUST

When creating a charitable trust, you must choose between *a Charitable Remainder Annuity Trust (CRAT) or a Charitable Remainder Unit Trust (CRUT).*

CRATS must pay *either* a fixed amount of dollars out of income and, if income is insufficient, out of principal; or must pay a fixed percentage out of the initial fair market value of assets transferred to the trust and, if income is insufficient, out of principal.

Once the dollar payout is set, it is fixed for the trust term and no subsequent reevaluations are made. Any excess income is retained in the trust and added to the principal.

CRUTS will pay either:
1.   A fixed percentage of net fair market value of trust assets, revalued annually, out of income, and if income is insufficient, out of principal.
2.   Or the lesser of either of number (1) or the actual trust income. Deficiencies in distributions are made up in any later year when trust income exceeds the payout for the year.
3.   Or, the lesser of (1) or the actual trust income. Deficiencies in distributions *are not made up in later years.*

For any of the three, excess income is retained in the trust and added to the principal.

Regardless if you create either a CRUT or a CRAT, the obligation to pay the pre-set amount begins the day the trust is created and funded.

TAX BYPASS INSURANCE TRUSTS

I know what you are going to say - "I don't want anything with the word *insurance* in the name." And in many cases, I might agree. But if you have estate tax problems, and you want to keep what you made, read on!

Keep in mind once the value of your estate exceeds $600,000, the estate tax must be paid within nine months or the IRS will gladly sell your assets for you.

When you create an insurance trust you set up an ***Irrevocable Trust.*** The only thing you place in this trust is a life insurance policy. The irrevocable trust would consist of the you, the insured, the trustee and the beneficiary.

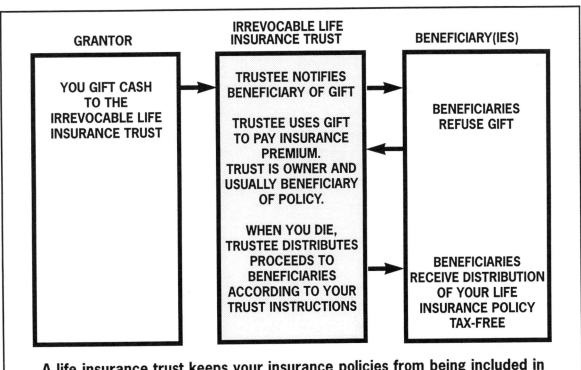

GRANTOR	IRREVOCABLE LIFE INSURANCE TRUST	BENEFICIARY(IES)
YOU GIFT CASH TO THE IRREVOCABLE LIFE INSURANCE TRUST	TRUSTEE NOTIFIES BENEFICIARY OF GIFT TRUSTEE USES GIFT TO PAY INSURANCE PREMIUM. TRUST IS OWNER AND USUALLY BENEFICIARY OF POLICY. WHEN YOU DIE, TRUSTEE DISTRIBUTES PROCEEDS TO BENEFICIARIES ACCORDING TO YOUR TRUST INSTRUCTIONS	BENEFICIARIES REFUSE GIFT BENEFICIARIES RECEIVE DISTRIBUTION OF YOUR LIFE INSURANCE POLICY TAX-FREE

A life insurance trust keeps your insurance policies from being included in your taxable estate and is one of the least expensive ways to pay estate taxes.

For married couples, the type of insurance purchased through the trust is usually called *Second-To-Die Insurance.* Meaning the proceeds (death benefit) would be paid after the death of the second spouse. As a result, the mortality tables are combined and the costs is less expensive.

Since the irrevocable trust is the owner, the insurance is not figured into your estate upon the second death. Rather, it will immediately be paid to your beneficiaries, avoiding your estate. Earlier I said, "If you don't need insurance, get rid of it." Now I am saying that if you are going to pay taxes, insurance could work, but only if it does not increase the value of your estate. Remember, I mentioned in the first chapter that when determining your net worth you should include insurance. That's now how you want it in this case. But you can have insurance that will not increase the value of your estate for tax purposes.

For example, assume both you and your wife are 65 years of age. Assume your estate is worth $900,000 and is growing at 6% per year. In 20 years your estate would be worth $2,000,000. You have created a revocable A/B trust providing protection from estate taxes up to $1,200,000. Now that your estate is worth $2,000,000, you don't feel it is right to give all that back to Uncle Sam, and you want to leave it to your children.

Based on $2,000,000, assume that you will owe $400,000. Create an insurance trust so your son and daughter will be the trustees. You and your spouse are the insured. Assume the insurance on $400,000 will cost $4,000 per year for the next twenty years. In total, you pay $80,000. You and your spouse pass away in 20 years, the insurance benefit bypasses your estate, and is paid directly to your children free of taxes and expenses. The $400,000 is then given to Uncle Sam and your estate tax paid for by the insurance has cost you only $80,000 instead of $400,000.

Now I have heard all the arguments -- "Let the kids pay the taxes," "Insurance is a bad investment," "I can do better in other investments," or "I will spend down the estate."

But seriously, analyze this approach. In the above example, it cost $80,000 over 20 years to get back $400,000. Not counting the value of money over time, your return on the investment was about 13% – *tax free!* Shop around and make sure it is a good investment but don't close your mind to the idea.

LOOK AT WHAT THE DIFFERENCE CAN BE BETWEEN THE TWO ESTATES WORTH $1,200,000:

WITHOUT LIFE INSURANCE TRUST		WITH LIFE INSURANCE TRUST
$1,200,000	Net worth (assets less debts)	$1,200,000
+ 400,000	Life insurance you own	+ 00
$1,600,000	Net estate	$1,200,000
- 153,000*	Federal estate taxes	- 00**
$1,447,000	Balance	$1,200,000
+ 00	Proceeds from insurance trust	+ 400,000
$1,447,000	Amount in assets for beneficiaries	$1,600,000

* Taxes with an A/B living trust. Otherwise you would pay an additional $255,000 in estate taxes

** Taxes with an A/B living trust. Otherwise you would pay $235,000 in estate taxes.

Although there are many arguments and reasons to utilize a life insurance trust, you can put everything else aside and look at this very simply. If you are single and have an estate over $600,000, or think you will in the near future, you will pay estate taxes. Will the insurance trust save you money? Is it a good investment? The same is true if you are married and have an estate over $1,200,000. In addition, life insurance proceeds are available soon after death. If your estate is liquid you might not receive the full value of the estate.

Remember to make certain that the proceeds from the insurance (death benefit) are not included in the gross value of your estate as the trustee of your insurance trust. Perhaps the same person that is the trustee of your living trust can be the trustee. There are also institutional trust companies or bank that will administrate the trust for a fee. Be clear that as a result of not being the trustee, and because this is in an irrevocable trust, you do lose control. Because of this, be certain to set forth strict provisions in the trust so that the trustee administers your wishes exactly as you desire.

In addition, you might want to make the ***Irrevocable Insurance Trust*** the beneficiary of the insurance policy instead of the children. If you leave it to the children, again you lose control. They might decide not to use the insurance to pay the estate taxes or might take cash value from the insurance policy. If you have a separate trustee and the trust is also the beneficiary, these potential problems are greatly reduced if not eliminated. You set forth in the trust document that the trustee is to utilize the insurance proceeds to first pay any taxes owed upon your death.

Finally, be sure that *neither you nor your spouse pay one penny of the insurance premium.* If you do, the policy might be considered as a part of the total value of your estate. As discussed previously, you are allowed to gift $10,000 per year per person ($20,000 for married couples). So gift $10,000 per beneficiary of the trust. But give the money to the trustee. The beneficiaries must sign a special provision called a ***Crummy Provision.*** In layman's terms, this states that the beneficiary *willingly forfeited* the gift to be used for the purposes of the insurance premium inside the trust.

HERE'S HOW MUCH IT WILL COST A $3 MILLION ESTATE TO PAY ESTATE TAXES, DEPENDING ON THE TAX PLANNING OPTION USED:

1. Using the Marital Deduction, no estate taxes are due when the first spouse dies; but when the second spouse dies, $1,098,000, or 37% of the estate, would be consumed by estate taxes.

2. An A/B living trust protects $1.2 million, but that still leaves $784,000 in estate taxes, or 26% of the estate.

3. Combining an A/B living trust with a life insurance trust reduces the cost of paying the $784,000 in estate taxes to only $122,000, just 4% of the estate's value. That's approximately how much it costs to purchase $784,000 in life insurance*. That's a 6.5 to 1 ratio – every dollar spent on insurance premiums pays $6.50 in estate taxes!

* Actual premium (for a male age 60 and female at 58), is $122,552 and is for a second-to-die policy, all whole life, from an AAA-rated insurance company.

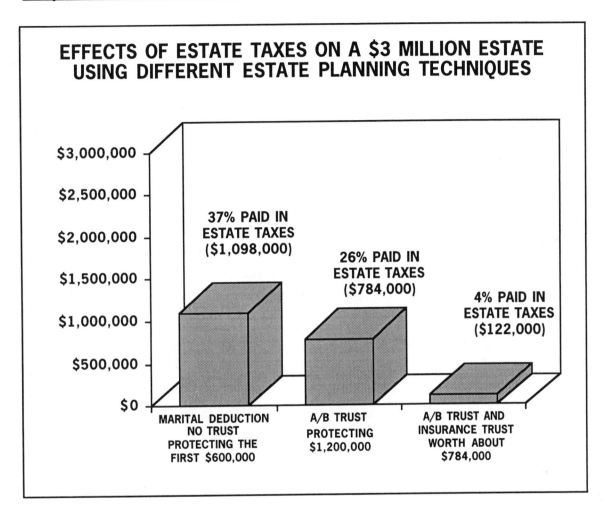

LIFE ESTATE

A *Life Estate* is the right to use, possess, or enjoy the property and the income it produces for as long as the holder of the life estate lives. The person holding title to the remainder interest owns the balance of the interest in the property not held by the life tenant. A life estate is when someone wishes to gift a home to someone else, but retain all rights and access to the home. Upon death of the life tenant the ownership of the property reverts to the holder of the remainder interest. Benefits include the fact that Medicaid cannot get to your asset (but watch out for the 30-month look-back rule). The house will also pass probate-free.

Another advantage of a life estate is that the property will still receive a step-up in basis for tax purposes. Upon the owner's death, the value of the property will equal the tax basis. For example, assume you purchase a home for $50,000 and subsequently entered into a life estate for the property with your son. Twenty years later, you pass away and the value of the home is $150,000. The tax basis of the property is no longer $50,000, it is $150,000.   In theory, your son can sell the property for $150,000 the next day and not owe capital gains tax. Obviously, this is a better technique than simply selling the home to your son during your lifetime because of capital gains tax your son will owe upon the sale of the property.

One possible downside to creating a life estate is the fact that since the property is technically yours, you have not made a gift. As a result, you cannot reduce the value of your estate by the value of the home that was placed in the life estate. The problem arises when your estate is over $600,000 and you are searching for ways to reduce the value of your estate for tax purposes. This technique will not help you in that endeavor.

WHAT SHOULD YOU DO?

1. If you have not used your Section 121, use it to eliminate up to $125,000 of capital gains tax on your personal residence. All the normal Section 121 requirements must be met.

2. Use your lifetime exclusion of $600,000 while you're alive. Most people don't use it before their death, but if your estate is presently valued at $600,000 and you believe it will stay there, use the exclusion.

3. If worse comes to worst and this is the best scenario, pay the tax.

One last point – if all criteria are followed, by creating a life estate you may be able to protect the assets from creditors such as Medicaid.

PRIVATE ANNUITIES

A private annuity is an agreement that you would enter into directly with another person or entity. There is no insurance company involvement. Seniors usually use this planning technique to get assets out of their names but retain the income for life.

The following is a good example of a private annuity: Mr. and Mrs. Jones want to give their son John $500,000. Let's assume the cost basis of the $500,000 gift is $200,000, meaning they have an imputed capital gain of $300,000. Based on their life expectancy and a 7% interest rate, their son would make annual payments of $44,927 to the parents.

For the parents, $7,042 of that annual payment over 28 years represents the recovery of the original costs of the business and would not be taxable. Capital gain would include $10,563 and $27,321 would be considered ordinary income. If Mr. and Mrs. Jones died in a few years, the son's obligation would end upon the death of both parents and the value of the son's annuity is not included in the value of his parents' estate. One can also structure the annuity to end payments after a set number of years.

This strategy can work for assets such as businesses, real estate or stocks. The problem is the capital gains tax that the recipient will pay when it is time to sell. That is the reason the private annuity works best with gifts of cash.

The down side for the donors is if the recipient is unable or refuses to make payments, or if the recipient is sued. The donor could lose his stream of income.

As discussed in many other chapters, you can create an annuity. Many people have been placing assets in a private account, making the children the owner and beneficiary, however, you would be the annuitant -- whereas you receive all income, they receive all benefits related to the principal and will receive the asset, probate free upon death. The advantage is almost the same as the life estate. It is out of your estate, and no one can touch your principal (creditors or Medicaid), but you cannot touch it either. All the other obstacles discussed under life estate apply to private annuities.

> **It is only a gift if you make someone else the owner and yourself the annuitant. This is not the same as using annuities to protect from Medicaid or using annuities as an investment.**

FAMILY LIMITED PARTNERSHIPS

This strategy is, arguably, the most complicated of all the above strategies. The following overview is very simplified. Consult a professional to discuss your particular situation.

You might look at *Family Limited Partnerships* if you want to reduce the value of your estate, (preferably by giving assets to family members), and you want to avoid losing assets to Medicaid or creditor claims. Most importantly, you wants to keep full control of the asset.

Through a family limited partnership you place the assets in the name of the limited partnership. Then you issue shares of ownership, have voting rights and nominate the general partner. The general partner (creator) has all voting rights and management decisions but the limited partners have none. However, you give the limited partners the majority ownership, and you, the general partner, very little.

For example, let's say you have $1,000,000. You create a family limited partnership making you and your spouse general partner and owner of 10% of the shares. Your stock as general partner is the only voting stock allowing you full control to invest the assets as you see fit. All your other beneficiaries will receive the remaining 90%.

Technically the other 90% is not in your name and is inaccessible to creditor claims It is not included in the value of your estate and you're not taxed. As general partner, you will be in charge of calculating the income and figuring the tax benefits or burden. A K-1 tax form would have to be sent to all the limited partners. Although you, as the general partner, are in charge and control of all the assets, you don't pay any taxes on the other limited partners' shares.

The point to be concerned about is how to transfer assets from your estate to the partnership. Again, the gifting rules may apply causing a burden on the taxes. If you sell the investments before transferring the property, you could be subject to a capital gain. Review the same considerations under life estate.

CHAPTER 12

What To Do When
Your Spouse Dies

Although I am not a physician, I think the period immediately after a spouse's death should be a time to grieve, not worry about financial problems. Hopefully, if the other chapters are utilized correctly in this book, you should be well prepared in the event of a spousal death.

First and foremost, make sure you are clear about your loved one's funeral wishes (i.e., cremation, burial). A good funeral director can handle most of the arrangements. *Remember to have someone stay home during the funeral because burglars read obituaries!*

After the funeral review your document locator. This paper is something everyone should have filled out in its entirety. You should have all the names and numbers of your attorneys, accountants and financial planner. You should also list all of your assets and where original documents can be found (i.e., a stock certificate held at the company, or a bond certificate in the safe deposit box). Also, when you list your assets, make a note as to how title is held, such as *Joint Tenant With Right Of Survivorship (JTWROS)*, or in the name of the *Family Trust.* The document locator should also show all sources of income, and you should know what happens to your spouse's income after death. (Is it reduced or eliminated?) Once you have thoroughly reviewed the contents of the document locator, the following would be a process to make sure everything is handled in a timely fashion.

Before you begin, make sure that you obtain several certified copies of death certificates. Either the funeral director or county clerk's office will have these. Whatever the amount you think would be enough – double it, then you should have enough – at least 15 copies. A marriage certificate and birth certificates for both you and the deceased spouse may be necessary as well. If you have to go through probate they will be required.

WHAT TO DO FIRST IF YOUR SPOUSE DIES

1.   Request any insurance proceeds.

First call the companies with which you hold the insurance. Tell them the circumstance, and ask how to proceed. Provided you are the beneficiary, they will request a copy of the death certificate before releasing any of the proceeds.

2.   Go through all retirement income sources.

These may be from a military pension, work pension, Social Security and whatever else. Obviously, if the check is made payable to the spouse, you cannot cash it. Call the various entities paying this income and ask them what is the procedure regarding a death and what you are supposed to do. Compare your records to the information you are given. Your spouse might have elected *full retirement benefits to spouse* after the worker's death. Always save the paper stating this because even big companies make big mistakes. Regarding Social Security benefits, first decide whose income is more, and select that one -- you cannot take both.

3.   Change the name on all your assets.

4.   Contact an attorney.

If assets are in separate names, and/or a valid will exists and it is necessary to obtain assets, contact an attorney. Your attorney will file the will in court and then try to get on the docket as soon as possible. This could be a long, tedious process, so be patient.

5.   Contact your accountant to provide a final tax return.

If you did not go through probate, and an audit or appraisals were not performed at this point, the IRS may do a final audit. Your accountant may suggest you appraise certain assets as well. Remember, if you own a piece of real estate (your house), for IRS purposes, you will need to know the appraised value at the time of death. If the estate owes taxes it must be paid within nine months. And the income taxes must be filed by April 15th.

6.   While you are waiting for insurance money or probate to finish, adjust your financial plan.

Calculate your new monthly income and see if it is higher or lower. Review your expenses and decide if you are spending more or less money. Then readjust your plan accordingly. If your estate is now substantially larger, review gifting techniques and ways to shelter from estate taxes. If you will need more income, determine how much principal you can use each year and still be fairly certain you will not run out of money. If a large insurance sum is coming, make sure you are very clear on how to invest the money. Even if you are not entirely clear, simply put the funds in a money market and take your time reviewing options. At this point you may also want to plan your strategy regarding your demise -- how to make it easier on your beneficiaries -- and how they can avoid probate.

7.   Make sure the last expenses of your spouse are bona fide.

Many bills are sent that are simply a scam. It may look like a medical bill or something official but don't believe it until you have thoroughly researched it. *Along the same lines, many hospital and doctor bills are incorrect. I have heard that they are incorrect more than 60% of the time and most often in their favor.* Check and research every bill and argue it if you must. If your spouse did all the work on your estate and this business is new to you, enlist a professional to help you. Many attorneys, financial planners and estate planners are very competent and will be able to assist you. Most professionals will grant you a free initial consultation. Don't settle on the first one -- interview at least three, take copious notes, write all your questions down and ask them to each candidate. Call each back if you must.

ASSETS IN A REVOCABLE TRUST

If your assets are in the name of the trust, do not change the name. Remember that the trust is like a corporation, so just because one of the officers (trustees) has died does not mean you have to change the name of the corporation. If you have a trust you might want to notify all the places where you have assets by sending a certified letter. In the letter state that the other trustee has died and you would like his or her name removed as co-trustee of the trust. Have the letter *Signature-Guaranteed* (a brokerage firm or bank can provide this service), and send a certified copy of the death certificate with it. Make sure you see your accountant. It is very important as to what type of trust you have (revocable, A/B), if a irrevocable trust, or if you are the trustee. Make sure a visit to your estate planning accountant is one of the first steps you take.

ASSETS IN JOINT TENANCY WITH RIGHT OF SURVIVORSHIP (JTWROS)

If your assets are in joint tenancy with right of survivorship they will not go through probate and the survivor *will not owe an immediate tax.* After the death of the remaining spouse, taxes will be owed. (See the section on Joint Tenancy.) *Accounts will not be frozen,* and you should be able to carry on changing the assets in you name with little resistance.

The assets should be transferred to your name only. This is done by sending the certified, signature-guaranteed letter requesting the removal of the joint tenant. The death certificate will be required.

ASSETS IN JOINT TENANCY AS COMMUNITY PROPERTY

Very similar to that of assets as JTWROS. The major difference being after second death, taxes are not owed on most assets as a result of the automatic step up in tax basis.

Warning: Be careful of putting someone else's name on your property, including your children. After one spouse dies, the survivor will often put children and other beneficiaries on title with them. This is not recommended for several reasons:

1.   You may be giving a gift over the yearly $10,000 allowed and as a result you could owe gift taxes.

2.   You lose control. If you put your son on property with you, and if your son goes through bankruptcy or gets sued you are jeopardizing your property. Furthermore, if your son is married, his wife's signature may be required as well as his when you decide to do sell or refinance the property.

CHAPTER 13

Senior Specialties

Although we spend so much money in taxes, I don't think it is all bad. There are so many services, federal and state programs available for mature Americans that you know your tax dollars are going to worthwhile programs. It is a shame that public awareness of these programs are lacking and needs to be better communicated.

Under the section on taxes we listed all the telephone numbers and special programs designed for seniors.

Your local *Area Agency For the Aging* is an excellent source of advice and knowledge. Chances are if they do not have the answer to your question, they will know where to find it. The services they provide are almost all encompassing and should be utilized. See the appendix for national Area Agencies for the Aging.

Another misunderstood area is insurance. This might include disagreements with Medicare, how to choose a good Medicare supplement, what to do if you feel and insurance agent was not clear. These problems should not be dealt with alone. Call the State Insurance Commissioner and ask what help is available in your area. Many volunteer counselors even come to your home. Many states will have organizations that will help you dispute Medicare claims, help choose a Medicare supplement, or a number of other services. All at very little or no cost.

Also, many states have legal services for senior citizens. For little or no cost they may provide you with legal services, such as a will, power-of-attorney, quitclaim deed, homesteading, conservatorship actions or Medicaid counseling. To find out about these services call the State Bar Association, or the local Area Agency for the Aging.

Other wonderful services include the hospice program, active lobbyists, caregiver associations and so many more it would be hard to name them all.

In addition, many retirees are now facing the problem of caring for their elderly parents. I have found that the following agencies can help you:

HELPFUL AGENCIES:

National Association of Professional Geriatric Care Managers   **(602) 881-8008**

They help provide the names of private care managers in all parts of the country.

National Academy of Elder Law Attorneys   **(602) 881-4005**

They will provide referrals for attorneys in estate and Medicaid planning.

Health Information Center   **(800) 336-4797**

They help in a wide variety of medical problems and an excellent source for referrals.

Alzheimer's Disease and Related Disorders Association   **(800) 621-0379**
(800) 527-6037 In Illinois

The Dependent Care Connection Employee Counseling Services   **(203) 226-2680**

WHERE SHOULD YOU LIVE DURING YOUR RETIREMENT?

Although you might not be thinking about finances when you decide to pick the area that you will live during your retirement, you should be. One of the biggest costs in retirement could be the taxes associated with the area where you live. State and local taxes vary widely. By being a senior citizen, most states will give you a break but the amounts can differ like night and day.

You really have to write down all the taxes and weigh your options. Seven states have no state taxes, and five states have no sales tax. However, fifteen states tax Social Security benefits. Since many of these states are not the same, it is difficult to really determine the best state for you.

The most generous states exclude all pension income from taxation. These states include Alabama, Hawaii, Illinois and Pennsylvania. States that tax all of your pension income include Connecticut, Rhode Island and Vermont.

The next big tax includes property tax. Forty-eight states and the District of Columbia grant property tax relief to elderly homeowners and/or renters. This is accomplished through state-financed circuit-breakers or homestead exemptions. The circuit-breaker, property taxes (or rent equivalents) are reduced through a state-financed credit or rebate when they exceed specified percentages of household income. With a homestead exemption, a specific dollar amount is subtracted from the assessed property value, thus lowering the mature homeowner's taxes. The states that offer no property relief on taxes include Florida, Louisiana, Michigan, Minnesota, Oregon, Vermont and Wisconsin.

We have discussed estate taxes in great detail and most of the tax figures discussed the federal tax. However, 17 states also tax inheritance. Another six states have a state tax on estates over and above the federal tax.

STATES THAT EXCLUDE ALL PENSION INCOME FROM TAXATION
Alabama, Hawaii, Illinois, Pennsylvania

STATES THAT HAVE NO STATE INCOME TAX
Alaska, Florida, Nevada, South Dakota, Texas, Washington, Wyoming

STATES THAT HAVE NO SALES TAX
Alaska, Delaware, Montana, New Hampshire, Oregon

STATES THAT TAX ONLY INTEREST AND DIVIDENDS
New Hampshire, Tennessee

STATES THAT TAX ALL OF YOUR PENSION INCOME
Connecticut, Rhode Island, Vermont

STATES THAT OFFER NO PROPERTY TAX RELIEF
Florida, Louisiana, Michigan, Minnesota, Oregon, Vermont, Wisconsin

STATES THAT TAX YOUR SOCIAL SECURITY BENEFITS
Colorado, Connecticut, Iowa, Kansas, Minnesota, Missouri, Montana, Nebraska, New Mexico, North Dakota, Rhode Island, Utah, Vermont, West Virginia, Wisconsin

---

As you can see, with all the different possible taxes and tax breaks, it is very difficult to "compare apples to apples." I would advise outlining where you think you might live and the call or write the local Congressman and Chamber of Commerce. Ask specific questions regarding taxation and obtain a state return form. You may consider completing that state's tax return as if you and your spouse are living and after death to get an understanding of their tax implications. There is also a book available from Commerce Clearing House called, *The State Tax Handbook* that might help you with your decision.

CHOOSING ADVISORS

Regardless of the complexity of your situation, the size of your estate, amount of your own involvement, it is prudent that you have advisors working for you on your behalf. I call this your Board of Advisors. You should enlist the services of three different professionals to create your Board and they would include an accountant, an attorney and a financial planner.

AN ACCOUNTANT

An accountant will serve several purposes during your retirement and beyond. You must find an accountant who knows how to prepare a tax return, understands the special needs of senior citizens, understands trusts and is very proficient in preparing final tax returns and trust tax returns.

The first step to finding a good accountant is to ask your friends for references. Perhaps the best suggestions could come from the others on your Board, the attorney or the financial planner. Interview at least three potential candidates before making a selection. If you feel pressure or too much eagerness from a candidate, listen to the warning signals.

Check their credentials. Obviously the most widely known is the *Certified Public Accountant (CPA)* although the *Enrolled Agent* designation (EA) is becoming more popular.

Have a list of prepared questions ready for your interview. If the accountant does not answer them to your satisfaction, scratch off that candidate.

QUESTIONS YOU CAN ASK AN ACCOUNTANT:

1. How many final tax returns have you completed?
2. How long have you been in practice?
3. What is your area of expertise?
4. What is your fee schedule? (Be careful if they charge by the hour without having a cap on their fees.)
5. What is the cost of a phone call?
6. What is the cost of a consultation?
7. What is the cost for the yearly returns and booking?

Also, ask his/her opinion regarding some general questions. If the accountant knows the rules, he/she should give you a definite answer. If he/she doesn't, he/she may offer vague answers or information. Perhaps a good general question would be, "What is involved after the first death in completing a tax return for the 'B' side of a trust?"

Get references. In order to avoid them giving you a "good buddy" reference, when I ask for references, I specifically ask for people who have my zip code, or ask for three references with the last names beginning with each of the letters A, B and C. If they cannot produce a reference for each, their client list may not be extensive. Also ask for one or two professional references.

THE FINANCIAL PLANNER

The financial planner is an essential member for your Board. A good planner will know many of the general guidelines regarding the plans made by your attorney and your accountant and be available to explain them to you. He/She will advise you and suggest what your attorney and accountant should be doing in your behalf.

Unfortunately, it is harder to determine who is a good financial planner because almost anyone can call himself/herself a financial planner. An important credential to look for is *Certified Financial Planner (CFP)*. This is the industry's certification necessary to understand true financial planning because it involves lengthy training followed by a difficult exam.

Many times a financial planner will be licensed to transact security business. This is a plus because this planner can help your transfer assets, choose various components of your plan and help with your investment choices. If the financial planner is registered to transact security business you will see "member of the National Association of Security Dealers (NASD), and Securities Investors Protection Corporation (SIPC)" on his/her business card. The NASD is the self-regulatory body of securities dealers, very much like the bar association is to attorneys. They police the organization in order to detect and prevent unscrupulous or unfair practices. Ask the planner for his/her CRD number, which is the identification number with the NASD. You can call your local NASD branch, give them the ID number and ask how long the candidate has been licensed, if there are any pending or past lawsuits against this planner, and what the outcome was. Be very careful if you find your candidate is not a member of the NASD.

Before engaging his/her services you should ask any candidate to prepare a letter regarding what he/she envisions for your financial plan and how his/her expertise will help.

Ask him/her to be very specific. Many planners will do this for no charge. Some may be leery that you will use this information to forward to another planner, so he/she will charge you a nominal fee. Most planners are willing to do the preliminary work for little or no fee to "show you what they've got." But you make the decision. A good financial planner is well worth the money.

After you feel comfortable with your planner's qualifications, you need to know about compensation. Some planners charge an hourly fee, others charge yearly rates. If he/she is charging a fee, make sure he/she does not receive a commission as well. Ask for a letter stating that all investments and insurance recommended and used in your plan are purchased on a no load, no commission basis. And be sure to get this in writing. Also, ask if there is a cap (maximum) on his/her fees, and after a certain numbers of hours, if there is a fee reduction.

I do not oppose fee planning because the investor will know that the planner is not making decisions based on sales. Some commission-paid planners are great but it is more difficult for you to discern and regulate.

If a planner charges a commission, your questions should be more along the lines of, "Show me two choices for every investment or strategy you suggest. What is the commission for each? What is the performance of the investment or insurance after the commission is deducted?"

Some investors will argue that it is actually better using a financial planners who earn commissions rather than charge fees. This rationale is based on the fact that many investment products enjoy the same performance as non-commission products, net of commission. So, if you do not have to pay a fee out of pocket, your investments will perform the same as non-commissioned products and you are actually receiving the services cheaper. However, it is difficult to regulate. You must find a good planner because what incentive does the planner have to continue doing actual planning work if no commissions are to be earned? Some planners feel the commission justifies the ongoing planning work, and if the client does not stay pleased, he/she may lose the client's business. This may be true, but it is you who must ultimately decide.

THE ATTORNEY

The selection of an attorney is an extremely important decision. Follow the same steps used for the other two advisors, including calling client and professional references. If you are looking for an estate planning attorney, it is important to peruse sample trust documents. Questions to ask would include how long has this been the attorney's area of expertise and what were the results of prior similar cases.

Call the Bar Association in your state to check on the attorney. Ask the length of time the attorney has had his or her license, if any complaints have been registered and if there are any lawsuits pending against him or her.

During the interview ask the attorney what part of the law is his or her specialty. In this day and age seniors need advisors who specialize. How could a lawyer be an expert at worker's compensation and estate planning at the same time? The amount of experience, knowledge and continuous education required for estate planning is enormous. Also ask if he or she is a member of the Estate Planning Section of the Bar Association. Perhaps you might even call the attorney's office anonymously and see if they would take a case in another area or refer you elsewhere.

You must create a competent team in your Board of Advisors. You can always make alterations but don't put it off any longer. By taking no action at all to establish your Board, you could be causing your estate much harm.

PART THREE

HEALTH CARE PLANNING

CHAPTER 14

Medicare, HMOs and Nursing Homes

Medicare is the current federal health care insurance system that most people over the age of 65 receive. Medicare will pay for certain medical-related claims of qualified recipients.

HOW DO I GET MY MEDICARE CARD? WHAT DEPARTMENT ADMINISTERS MEDICARE?

Medicare is administered by the Health Care Financing Administration, which is within the Department of Health and Human Services.

Usually three months prior to age 65, you should go to your local Social Security Administration office. Once there you will complete an application for Medicare and then receive the basic information. Within the next two or three months you should receive the Medicare card that should be kept with you at all times. Make copies and put the copies in your safety deposit box.

WHO QUALIFIES FOR MEDICARE BENEFITS?

Usually all persons 65 or older who are eligible for Social Security benefits are eligible for Medicare benefits.

WHAT MEDICAL EXPENSES DOES MEDICARE COVER?

Medicare is divided into two parts, Medicare Part A and Medicare Part B.

Part A is free to everyone eligible for Medicare benefits. Medicare Part B is voluntary insurance coverage that you may agree to pay for as well. The way it usually works, is that when you enroll in Medicare, you are automatically signed up for Part B as well. If you do not want Part B, you must instruct the officers in writing to omit you from enrollment. If you do not, your Social Security check will automatically pay Part B for you. Currently the cost for Part B is $31.80 per month although the costs rise every year.

MEDICARE PART A

Medicare Part A covers mostly hospital-related claims. Although there are enormous deductibles, it will pay most of the first 60 days in a hospital. From the 61 days to 90 days in a hospital, they will pay any costs over the $163 per day.

MEDICARE PART A: HOSPITAL INSURANCE

Medicare's Benefits and Exclusions[1]

Service	Medicare Benefits	Your Costs
Hospitalization	• Full cost after deductible is met (1st-60th day)	• $652 per benefit period in 1992[2]
	• Full cost after co-insurance (61st-90th day)	• $163 per day co-insurance in 1992
	• Full cost after co-insurance for 60 lifetime reserve days, OR	• $326 per day co-insurance in 1992
	• $0 after 60 reserve days are used.	• Full cost

Post-hospital care in a certified skilled-nursing facility (SNF)	• 100% of approved amounts for the first 20 days of care each benefit period after 3-day hospital stay	• $0
	• Full cost after co-insurance (21st-100th day)	• $81.50 per day co-insurance in 1992
	• $0 after 100th day	• Full cost
Intermediate and custodial nursing care	• $0	• Full cost
Home health care	• 100% of approved amount of Medicare-approved services	• $0
	• 80% of approved amount for durable medical equipment	• 20% of approved amount in 1992
Hospice	• All but limited costs for outpatient drugs and inpatient respite care	• Limited cost-sharing for outpatient drugs and inpatient respite care
Blood	• Full cost after first 3 pints	• First 3 pints[3]

[1] The information above is accurate as of January, 1992. It will change from year to year.

[2] Benefit period begins on the first day you receive services as an inpatient in a hospital and ends after you have been out of the hospital or skilled nursing facility for 60 days in succession.

[3] To the extent the blood deductible is met under one part of Medicare during a calendar year, it does not have to be met under the other part.

NURSING HOME CARE

Medicare may also pay for a portion of a skilled nursing home. Most people do not use skilled facilities because they handle patients with only the most severe ailments. Skilled care is defined as round-the-clock supervision requiring aid in handling routine daily activities such as eating, using bathroom facilities or administering medication. Medicare will only pay the amount over the first $81.50 per day if you meet certain criteria. You must have been hospitalized for at least three days immediately prior to entering the nursing home. Often patients in nursing homes do not come from a hospital.

HOSPICE CARE

This is one of the better services available to seniors. This may include services such as medical social services, home health-aid services, counseling, and therapy. The bad news is that in order to receive hospice care you must be terminally ill with a maximum life expectancy of six months. However, continuing services are provided to a survivor of the deceased. If your doctor or hospital does not properly educate you to the wonderful services offered by hospice, I encourage you to call your local hospice and ask them to send you some information.

HOME-HEALTH CARE

This is another fairly good service offered by Medicare. If a doctor prescribes treatment for intermittent home-health care this is a covered service. However the care must be part-time intermittent defined as care up to six days per week for up to three consecutive weeks. Treatment cannot take more than a total of 35 hours per week.

MEDICARE PART B

Medicare Part B is the optional part of Medicare. This is the coverage for a doctor's office visits. In all fairness, it is a good plan for the price. Unless you have a supplement provided by your previous employer that costs you very little, do not hesitate to have Part B as well. The outline of the coverage is as follows:

MEDICARE PART B: MEDICAL INSURANCE

Service	Medicare Benefits	Your Cost
Physician and surgical services, medical supplies, diagnostic tests, durable medical equipment	• 80% of approved amounts exceeding the annual deductible of $100	• $100 each year plus 20% of approved amounts plus additional amounts charged by doctors who do not accept assignment
Laboratory services: Blood tests, biopsies, etc.	• 100% of approved amounts	• $0

Home health care	• 100% of approved amounts for Medicare-approved services (no deductible)	• $0
	• 80% of approved amount for durable medical equipment (after deductible)	• 20% of approved amount
Outpatient hospital care	• 80% of approved amount (after deductible)	• 20% of approved amount
Blood	• 80% of approved amount after first 3 pints	• First 3 pints plus 20% of approved amount for additional pints (2)

DOCTORS` VISITS

Although many services are not covered, those covered include: surgery, consultation, diagnostic procedures that are part of your treatment, some medical supplies, medications, physical therapy, speech therapy, speech pathology and a myriad of other services. Some medical supplies and drugs, physical therapy and speech pathology. Even certain dental, psychiatric, and other specialties may be included.

OUTPATIENT HOSPITAL

Usually this covers services billed to the hospital such as x-rays, laboratory work or emergency services. A breakdown of costs is as follows:

DOCTORS` SERVICES

YOU PAY...	MEDICARE PAYS...
$100 DEDUCTIBLE.	**80% MEDICARE-APPROVED CHARGES**
20% MEDICARE-APPROVED CHARGES.	
100% NON-MEDICARE APPROVED CHARGES.	

APPROVED CHARGES

It is extremely important to understand what is meant by *Approved Charges.* If an overpriced doctor charges you $200 and the Medicare-approved charge for that service is $100 dollars, you may have to pay $20 for the first 20% deductible of the $100 that Medicare covers, and then 100% of the additional $100. Your total will be $120 of the $200 service.

To regulate approved charges, the *Health Care Financing Administration (HCFA)* started the process in January, 1992 of a five-year phase-in system. Prior to every January, starting in 1992, the HCFA establishes fee schedules to which physicians must adhere for all services covered under Medicare. However, there is much room for "interpretation" because the formula for a "reasonable" fee schedule is complicated.

Put as simply as possible, the formula must include the national uniform relative values for all physicians' services. The relative value of each service must be the sum of relative value units representing physicians' work, experience and the cost of malpractice insurance. The national uniform relative values are adjusted for each locality by a geographic adjustment factor.

Under this new system, chances are that Medicare payments will rise dramatically for primary care and cognitive services, but they should decline for procedure-based services. The payments for the family and general practitioners will also increase significantly. However, payments for surgical specialties will decrease. The bottom line is that new system will favor primary care and most rural areas. Conversely, the system will be penalizing specialized procedures and urban areas.

Even with the new system supposedly answering all questions regarding fees, in any system there will still be disputes and discrepancies regarding what is covered and the amount of coverage. You must learn how to properly dispute a ruling if you feel you have been charged incorrectly.

The new fee schedules and rules must be completely phased in by 1996. I hope this new system clarifies the old method of using "approved charges." However, I think this is a very difficult undertaking.

HOW TO FILE A CLAIM

You must submit a Medicare Payment Form, or 1490S. To file a claim, almost all Medicare doctor's offices, approved carriers, and Social Security offices have copies of this form. Often they will help you fill them out but the instructions on the back of the form are fairly clear.

For all Part B claims, the bills must be submitted by your doctor or Medicare carrier without charge.

The Medicare carrier (see appendix for list), will withhold the $100 deductible and pay 80% of the amount determined to be reasonable, the reasonable charges, or however the new fee schedule sets the charge. It will be your responsibility to pay the 20% difference plus 100% of the amount that was charged to you in excess of the "reasonable charge" that Medicare has outlined.

Usually, you pay your doctor the 20% that Medicare does not pay. Note that the doctor is not allowed to charge a patient more than the 20%. However, like any other business, some dishonest people will try to take advantage of senior citizens. Be careful and question everything!

You are entitled to an itemized bill that includes services rendered, health insurance claim number, description and charge for each service, and the doctor who performed the service. You may always appeal a Medicare decision by contacting the carrier in your state or the local Social Security office. Many states have Peer Review Organizations that you can utilize as well.

Common grounds for Medicare appeals usually arise as to whether or not a medical service was covered or with regard to the fee amount. Medicare will send you a statement reflecting how much was paid, if it was covered under Medicare and how to file a dispute. Remember, you are dealing with a bureaucracy. Disputing a claim is usually a long difficult process but persistence will be rewarded.

You are entitled a review of a claim handled by a Medicare carrier. You are required to send a written letter requesting reconsideration or review of a Medicare carrier that handled a claim. Send the letter to the Social Security Administration and the Health Care Financial Administration, you can receive a written review.

If you are not satisfied with the answer you receive from your written request, you can ask for a hearing with the Medicare carrier. You must submit the request for a hearing and file it with the same organizations where you filed your request for a review. Requests for either reviews or hearings must be made within six months after receiving the initial determination or the review determination.

Many individuals are also members of HMOs and other Medicare supplement organizations. Legally, you can appeal a decision made by the HMO. When you sign up to become a member of an HMO, they are required to give you, in writing, a full packet explaining exactly how you can initiate an appeal of a decision. In other words, don't throw your papers away!

WHAT MEDICARE DOESN'T COVER

Medicare does not cover a great deal. Obviously, it does not cover all the deductibles for doctors visits and hospital stays. But there are also many other health needs you may have that would not be covered.

First, don't forget the 20% of approved charges you have to pay. In addition, the doctor may have billed you for more then the approved charge.

Second, many dental, eye, prescription, and other health services are not included. You can get complete list from the Social Security Administration.

Third, and perhaps the most critical, Medicare rarely pays for any type of nursing home stay. They say they pay for "skilled" nursing care but they attach numerous caveats. Furthermore, most people that use nursing homes do not use "skilled" facilities. I have heard that, on the average, Medicare pays approximately only 2% of all claims for nursing homes.

If you are worried about paying all the things that Medicare does not cover, which could be a great deal, you might want to consider Medicare supplements.

MEDICARE SUPPLEMENTS

Medicare supplements are exactly that. They are supplemental insurance policies designed to pay for things Medicare will not. There are more supplements and types of supplements that you can buy, than you can count.

Under the new rules of the National Association of Insurance Commissioners (NAIC), effective in most states in and after 1992, there are now ten standard Medicare supplement policies. These policies are distinguished by the letters A through J. Although all states might not have all A through J options available the basic policy, Plan A, must be made available to Medicare recipients everywhere.

Basically, when shopping for a supplement, you should look for these qualities:

1.   COVERAGE

You should know exactly what it is you are buying. In my opinion, a good policy would pay all the co-insurance amounts. For example; if Medicare pays 80% and you pay 20%, the supplement should pay the 20%. If a doctor charges you over and above the "Medicare approved charge," the supplement should pay that amount. The supplement should, many times, pay for items not covered by Medicare. If Medicare will only pay for home-health care on a part-time, intermittent care for up to three weeks, the supplement might pay up to six weeks.

2.   QUALITY OF CARRIER

The quality of the carrier is one of the most important considerations in choosing a Medicare supplement. You should know what the insurance company is rated; AAA rating by Standard and Poor's is among the highest ratings issued. This is important, since your are paying the premiums you should know that the insurance company is going to be around for some years. You also want a company that has a good name in the Medicare supplement arena. Not necessarily a big name, but one that has proven to be excellent in supplements that pays most claims and pays them on time. An good statistic to ask a prospective insurance company is what percentage of claims they pay. Obviously 100% is unrealistic, but the higher, the better.

An interesting exercise would be to visit a library and research, through microfiche, all the articles written about the company you are thinking of using. This will give you an accurate, unbiased perspective of the pros and cons about that company. What have others said about it?

3.   TYPE OF FILING

Despite the fact they are trying to make the filing of Medicare claims easier, many times it is still not the greatest system. Some insurance companies that offer Medicare supplements have an electronic filing system. This means you do not have to make claims or sending anything to anyone. The doctor's office will simply do all the claims for you electronically. If you ever have tried to file claims or wait for reimbursement this is an advantage. Although 99% of the time it might go smoothly, it's that 1% when it doesn't go smoothly, that leaves the sour taste in your mouth. This is why electronic filing is a big advantage.

4. ACCESSIBILITY

This is important to make sure they have a good customer service department to call and ask questions. A toll-free number is always a plus. You might even try calling the home office to ask a question before you buy the insurance. When I get transferred on the phone to more than three people or if I am put on hold for more than three minutes, by that time I have decided I don't want that company handling my claims.

You also want to be sure that the doctors you use have heard of the company and do not have problems working with them. The last thing you want is to make life harder when you buy a supplement. If your doctor has trouble dealing with the company, think twice.

5. COST

You have heard the saying "if you buy a diamond for a dime, it is probably worth a dime." I found about the same is true when dealing with Medicare supplements. I have seen two different supplement policies with an almost 50% difference in price. On the surface it appears that the coverage is the same. Obviously it was not. And the cost for these polices can be extremely high. You first want to know if the premiums will rise as you get older, and by how much. You also want to know if you do have a claim as a result of a sickness or accident, will your cost go up, and by how much.

Another good exercise is to narrow your search down to three carriers without even looking at the price. Call all three carriers and ask for a "specimen policy." Read each one word for word. Don't take little seemingly non-relevant phrases for granted, such as "approved charges." Then you will have a better grasp on the best policy and how much it should cost.

One last point before actually purchasing the supplement is to ask about any "pre-existing condition" clauses. If, before you sign up, you had an operation on your back, will the policy you are about to buy exclude any coverage for your back? And if so, for how long?

Although supplements are wonderful, they are expensive and confusing. Do the research in advance of turning age 65, so you are not forced to rush into a policy.

STANDARD MEDIGAP PLANS

Following is a list of the ten standard plans and the benefits provided by each:

PLAN A (the basic policy) consists of these core benefits:

- Coverage for the Part A co-insurance amount ($169 per day in 1993) for the 61st day through the 90th day of hospitalization in each Medicare Benefit period.
- Coverage for the Part A co-insurance amount ($338 per day in 1993) for each of Medicare's 60 non-renewable lifetime hospital in-patient reserve days used.
- After all Medicare hospital benefits are exhausted, coverage for 100% of the Medicare Part A Eligible hospital expenses. Coverage is limited to a maximum of 365 days of additional in-patient hospital care during the policyholder's lifetime. This benefit is paid either at the rate Medicare pays hospitals under is Prospective Payment System or another appropriate standard of payment.
- Coverage under Medicare Parts A and B for the reasonable cost of the first three pints of blood or equivalent quantities of packed red blood cells per calendar year unless replaced in accordance with federal regulations.
- Coverage for the co-insurance amount for Part B series (generally 20% of approved amount) after $100 annual deductible is met.

PLAN B includes core benefits plus:

- Coverage for the Medicare Part A in-patient hospital deductive ($676 per benefit period in 1993).

PLAN C includes core benefits plus:

- Coverage for the Medicare Part A deductible.
- Coverage for skilled nursing facility care co-insurance amount ($84.50 per days for days 21 through 100 per benefit period in 1993).

- Coverage for the Medicare Part B deductible ($100 per calendar year in 1993).
- Coverage for medically necessary emergency care in a foreign country.

PLAN D includes core benefits plus:

- Coverage for the Medicare Part A deductible.
- Coverage for the skilled nursing facility care daily co-insurance amount.
- Coverage for medically necessary emergency care in a foreign country.
- Coverage for at-home recovery. The at-home recovery benefit pays up to $1,600 per year for short-term, at-home assistance with activities of daily living (bathing, dressing, personal hygiene, etc.) for those recovering from an illness, injury or surgery. There are various benefit requirements and limitations.

PLAN E includes core benefits plus:

- Coverage for the Medicare Part A deductible.
- Coverage for the skilled nursing facility care daily co-insurance amount.
- Coverage for medically necessary emergency care in a foreign country.
- Coverage for preventive medical care. The preventive medical care benefit pays up to $120 per year for such things as a physical examination, flu shot, serum cholesterol screening, hearing test, diabetes screenings and thyroid function test.

PLAN F includes core benefits plus:

- Coverage for the Medicare Part A deductible.
- Coverage for the skilled nursing facility care daily co-insurance amount.
- Coverage for the Medicare Part B deductible.
- Coverage for medically necessary emergency care in a foreign country.
- Coverage for 100% of Medicare Part B Excess charges.*

PLAN G includes core benefits plus:

- Coverage for the Medicare Part A deductible.
- Coverage for the skilled nursing facility care daily co-insurance amount.
- Coverage for 80% of Medicare Part B excess charges.*
- Coverage for medically necessary emergency care in a foreign country.
- Coverage for at-home recovery. (See Plan D.)

PLAN H includes core benefits plus:

• Coverage for the Medicare Part A deductible.

• Coverage for the skilled nursing facility care daily co-insurance amount.

• Coverage for medically necessary emergency care in a foreign country.

• Coverage for 50% of the cost of prescription drugs up to a maximum annual benefit of $1,250 after the policyholder meets a $250 per year deductible. (This is called the "basic" prescription drug benefit.)

PLAN I includes core benefits plus:

• Coverage for the Medicare Part A deductible.

• Coverage for the skilled nursing facility care daily co-insurance amount.

• Coverage for 100% of Medicare Part B excess charges.*

• Basic prescription drug coverage. (See Plan H for description.)

• Coverage for medically necessary emergency care in a foreign country.

• Coverage for at-home recovery. (See Plan D.)

PLAN J includes core benefits plus:

• Coverage for the Medicare Part A deductible.

• Coverage for the skilled nursing facility care daily co-insurance amount.

• Coverage for Medicare Part B deductible.

• Coverage for 100% Medicare Part B excess charges.*

• Coverage for medically necessary emergency care in a foreign country.

• Coverage for preventive medical care. (See Plan E.)

• Coverage for at-home recovery. (See Plan D.)

• Coverage for 50% of the cost of prescription drugs up to a maximum annual benefit of $3,000 after the policyholder meets a $250 per year deductible. (This is called the "extended" prescription drug benefit.)

*   Plan pays a specified percentage of he difference between the Medicare's approved amount or Part B services and the actual charges (up to the amount of charge limitations set by either Medicare or state law).

HEALTH MAINTENANCE ORGANIZATIONS

As stated in the previous chapter, the supplements can be very costly, sometimes too costly. A popular alternative for many people has been the *Health Maintenance Organizations (HMOs)*. The HMOs provide an excellent alternative to the high costs of private supplements. The down side is that you do not get to choose your own doctors. Many times you might not see the same doctor twice in a row.

If you don't mind the fact that you can't choose your doctor, then HMOs offer a great alternative. When reviewing the various HMOs available, go through the same check list you would in picking a Medicare supplement. Find out information such as costs and how they rise, coverage, the relationship to Medicare, and whether or not they pay for prescriptions.

In addition to the Medicare supplement check list, find out the locations of their various doctors and specialist. I have heard of cases where someone might have to drive over an hour to see the cardiac specialist. Although you might not have a heart problem now, you might one day and I am sure you will not want to drive an hour to see a doctor.

Ask about their policy on second opinions. If you are going to have a major operation, it is simply prudent to have a second opinion. If it is expensive, it is something that could affect your decision to use that HMO.

Some of the best research is had by asking friends what their experience has been -- are the doctors friendly, did they have to wait long, was the receptionist helpful, are the costs reasonable?

Regardless of whether or not you decide to utilize a private Medicare supplement or HMO, you still will not be covered for every contingency. One of the biggest costs facing mature Americans, and one of the hardest things to come to terms with, is the utilization of custodial care.

NURSING HOMES

The number of people using some type of assisted living is astronomical. A stay in a nursing home could turn a wealthy man into a pauper. Usually even the best of Medicare supplements or HMOs do not pay for over 100 days stay in a nursing home, and, again, so many restrictions apply that many times people pay for the care in a nursing home themselves, out of their own pockets.

I am sure you have said, or have heard, "I will never go into a nursing home." The numbers state otherwise and the numbers don't lie. You say you will not let it happen, but what if you have a stroke or acquire Alzheimer's and cannot make decisions? What if your spouse passes away and you do not have anyone to assist you? Whatever the reason, the numbers of people using some type of nursing care is growing astronomically and you are paying the high costs.

When we speak of nursing homes, it is important to remember that several kinds exist. The three most common include skilled care, intermediate care and custodial care.

- **SKILLED CARE:**

  This includes 24-hour supervision. A registered nurse is always on duty to administer prescription drugs, help with all facets of life including bathing, eating, or going to the bathroom. Ironically, this is the care that is least used (only by .5% of seniors), but the best covered by Medicare. This type of care would be for seniors with major incapacitating ailments, such as severe strokes.

- **INTERMEDIATE CARE:**

  This type of care might still have an RN on duty, but it is not for patients who require 24-hour supervision. But these patients do need more care than someone needing post-operative assistance. Approximately 4.5% of seniors use this care.

- **CUSTODIAL CARE:**

  This care is commonly used by seniors recovering from surgery, in the early stages of Alzheimer's, or who cannot take care of themselves alone. People here help with routine, daily activities. This is the care that is most used (almost 96%), but almost never covered by Medicare.

The costs of a nursing home are almost blinding, many times more than $150 per day, not including prescriptions or incidentals. It is estimated that half of the people who enter a nursing home are facing impoverishment within 13 weeks. If no one pays for this, what will you do? It's a tough question for any senior to answer.

A special Senate Committee on Aging Report showed the average person's health care costs are break as follows: $.19 on Medicare-eligible claims, and $.81 on Long-Term Care. Yes, statistics show we are growing older but they are not showing us that we are growing healthier as we age. Since October, 1993, nursing home admissions have risen by over 42%. Women tend to be the longest users of nursing home care.

Out of all the ingenious tricks that people have tried to use to get out of paying for a stay in a nursing home, three methods seem to make the most sense: Utilize a nursing home insurance plan, convert current life insurance into a special policy that will pay for a nursing home stay, or find a way to persuade Medicaid to pay.

USING A LONG-TERM CARE INSURANCE POLICY

I have no objection to someone using insurance to pay for a nursing home stay, if it is done properly. Too many people do not understand the coverage, do not understand what is involved, and by the time you need the coverage it is too late to correct the mistakes. The other problem is that the coverage can get to be quite expensive. It is not typically that expensive until you get into your middle sixties or early seventies, then watch out! *My advice is if you are going to get the coverage, stop procrastinating and get it while you are as young as possible and still eligible.*

To properly analyze an long-term insurance plan, these steps should be followed:

Call three companies and ask for sample policies. After receiving these sample policies you will be able to accurately research the next steps. Don't talk to an agent until you have narrowed down your options and have answered the following questions. It will, most likely, just confuse you.

ITEMS THAT SHOULD BE INCLUDED IN LONG-TERM HEALTH CARE INSURANCE POLICY BENEFITS:

1. Make sure insurance will pay the costs of an average stay in a nursing home.

2. Chances are you will not enter a care facility for many years, and by that time the costs will probably be even higher. Make sure the coverage you buy has an inflation rider.

3. Make sure the coverage would include payments to any type of care facility including skilled, intermediate, and custodial.

4. Make sure that you do not need to go directly from a hospital. Also make sure a doctor's prescription for entering a nursing home is not always necessary. Also as important, be clear that you can use this facility for physical and mental conditions, such as senility and Alzheimer's disease.

5. If you so desire, make sure you can acquire home-health care insurance as well.

6. Most people do not have overly long stays in convalescent facilities, so make sure you have the option of having the insurance start paying on the first day of entering a nursing home. In addition, you should know if your coverage pays for a set number of years or for your lifetime.

7. Make sure that your premium stops within a certain amount of time after you enter the care facility.

8. Find out if there is a pre-existing condition clause. If you had a back operation two years prior to buying the nursing home insurance, will they cover you to go into a nursing home because you are recovering from a back operation?

9. Make sure you know if your premium will ever increase and why. A good policy would not increase your premium just because you got older. Be certain your premium won't rise anytime you use a nursing home. Otherwise, your homecoming welcome after recovery might come in the form of a notice that your premiums are being increased.

Once you have these answers, then you can compare apples to apples. Look at the prices and see how they compare. As I suggested when discussing Medicare supplements, call the companies you are interested in to see how easy it is to get through and if they are courteous and helpful. Some great questions you might want to ask would include: What percentage of claims do you actually pay? What is your insurance company rating? This question is especially relevant as you may be relying on their payments many years in the future, you want to know if they will be around. Also, ask for a history showing every time they raised their premiums. This will give you a better handle on what is in store for you in the future.

In all fairness, if you can afford it, research this thoroughly. More and more seniors will be needing care and you are going to have to pay for it somehow.

CONVERTING A CURRENT LIFE INSURANCE POLICY TO PAY FOR NURSING HOME COSTS

As mentioned, the number of people using care is growing dramatically, and the costs are growing just as dramatically. Many creative insurance companies have come up with a possible solution. Convert your existing life insurance policies to special policies that will pay the cost of nursing home care when you need it.

This solution makes sense. The thought is this -- you currently have old insurance polices, each with a certain amount of cash value. You are at the point where you (or your spouse or beneficiaries) do not need the death benefit. Certain companies will transfer your cash value through a tax-free exchange into an new insurance policy that is designed to pay a certain amount of the death benefit to a nursing home should you need the care. If not, the death benefit would go to your spouse, or beneficiaries, as planned.

Obviously, this could be tricky, and may or may not make sense in your case. It is possible that the restrictions on actually using the money for a nursing home claim could be numerous or the death benefit might be significantly diminished. However, the benefits could be very rewarding.

MEDICAID

The last option that might pay for a nursing home stay is Medicaid. The good news is Medicaid will pay for a nursing home stay if you qualify. The bad news is that you have to be broke to qualify. The following chapter will explain this massive government health plan.

CHAPTER 15

Medicaid

WHAT IS MEDICAID?

Medicaid is a federal- and state-funded health insurance program for people who need financial aid for medical purposes. Although the various requirements and names might very from state to state, they are still part of the Medicaid system. In California, Medicaid is called MediCal. If, for example, you were in a Medicaid-approved facility, and you "qualified" for Medicaid, certain expenses for medical care would be paid.

HOW TO QUALIFY FOR MEDICAID

This is the tricky part. Technically, to qualify for Medicaid you must be impoverished. In 1989 the *Spousal Impoverishment Act* was passed. This federal act set the guidelines that limit the total income and assets of Medicaid recipients in care facilities and the assets and income of their spouses.

The act set forth a range of assets, each state has subsequently chosen the amounts in that range for their guidelines. Therefore all states are different. However, the two factors determining qualification are *household income* and *assets.*

FIRST TEST

Either you are in an ***Income Cap State or a Benefit State.*** An income cap state means that you cannot receive Medicaid for any reason if your income is over the set limit. A benefit state usually follows the same guidelines with one major exception -- if your income is over the limit amount, but less than the average cost of nursing homes in your area, they will still consider you for Medicaid eligibility.

In 1992, most states capped the well spouse's income to be eligible for Medicaid at approximately $1,266 per month although some states go to as much as $1,720 per month. And there will be an index for inflation on a yearly basis for these income levels.

PLAN AHEAD TO SET INCOME LOW IF NEED BE

If you plan ahead, you might be able to get your income low enough, and keep it low enough, to qualify for Medicaid.

PLAN AHEAD TO QUALIFY FOR MEDICAID

1. Take Social Security at 62 years of age to get the lower amount.

2. When you retire don't take a guaranteed income option, instead take the lump sum.

3. Invest in vehicles in which you can control income or those that do not have any income.

4. Move to a benefit state where the cost of nursing home is higher than your income.

The second test you must pass to qualify for Medicaid is the asset test.

SECOND TEST

The Spousal Impoverishment Act that went into effect in 1989 changed almost all the guidelines. The numbers vary from state to state, but minimum assets allowed are up to $13,700 in some states, with a maximum of $68,900 (based on 1992 numbers). These amounts increase each year. Still, without proper planning, the best that you can do is $68,900 (in 1992).

What this means is that, without planning, if either the sick or well spouse has over $68,900, neither will be eligible for Medicaid.

The creative person who plans ahead can avoid this. The best way is to convert all your assets over $68,900 (or whatever the maximum is for your state), to exempt assets.

EXEMPT ASSETS

An exempt asset is one that Medicaid does not include into the amount of assets allowed, and you can keep this asset even after applying and receiving Medicaid. Examples of exempt assets include:

1. YOUR PERSONAL RESIDENCE

A married couple owning a home will not have to include their residence in the Medicaid asset limitations. Most states do not stipulate the size of the home or dollar value. However, usually one spouse must still be living in the house to use it as an exempt asset. In addition, home furnishings, home improvements, and collectibles are usually exempt assets.

2. ONE CAR

Usually any dollar value.

3. IRREVOCABLE TRUSTS

If structured correctly, and in the proper time frame, the principal could be exempt in an irrevocable trust. A simple rule of thumb is, if you have no access to or control of the money, neither will Medicaid.

Usually a trust is *not* the best way to protect assets. A trust is a contract in which you, as creator, transfer an asset to another person. It is the other person's assignment as trustee to manage and oversee the funds in the best interests of the beneficiaries. A revocable trust is not effective because you, as creator, would probably be the trustee. As a result, when you have access to the funds, so does Medicaid and other creditors.

If you create an irrevocable fund and limit the amount of discretion given to the trustee (remember, you are *not* the trustee) the assets that you have placed in the trust can be protected. This means the trust must be set up *prior* to applying for Medicaid and the duties of the trustee must already be predetermined and will remain unchanged.

For example, income will be paid out of the trust for both lifetimes. When one spouse's illness requires long-term care, the income will only be paid to the healthy spouse. Upon the death of the second spouse, the trust terminates and the principal is distributed to the beneficiaries.

It is important to note that creating this type of trust and transferring assets to it will trigger the 30-month look-back rule and will disqualify that amount of the transfer from being eligible for Medicaid benefits. In other words, any assets transferred within 30 months of applying for Medicaid will be deducted. In addition and very important to understand is that once this trust is created, it cannot be altered or revoked in any way. It is why this type of trust is sometimes called a *Medicaid Trust or Medicaid Qualifying Trust.*

One of the major reasons that trust funds are protected is because of their inaccessibility. If you have no access to the principal or to the income, neither does Medicaid. Again, always be careful of the 30-month look-back rule.

4. PROPERLY STRUCTURED ANNUITIES AND/OR PRIVATE PENSION PLANS

An annuity is just a definition, just like a mutual fund. There are good and bad ones, safe and risky ones. If you wish, you can even create your own. The fact is, properly structured, an annuity can be a prudent way to protect your assets.

Now that you know the four general areas of protected assets, it is now a matter of how to use these exemptions to your benefit. The following strategies are some methods of protecting your assets:

1. **Pay off your home if a mortgage is still on it.** If the house is protected, why have unprotected cash in areas outside the house? If you pay off the mortgage the money will be sheltered. For that matter, you may consider purchasing a larger home. Remember, regardless of the size of the house, the asset is protected.

   If you need to make home improvements, need to buy new furnishings or jewelry (within limitations) these assets would also be exempt from Medicaid.

2. **Buy a new car.** If you are allowed one car, make sure you have a valuable new car.

3. **Protect your liquid cash and investments** by creating private pension plans or properly structured annuities.

ANNUITIES FOR MEDICAID PLANNING

Although it sounds complicated, create a *Personal Annuity or Private Pension Plan.* The process, handled by a professional, is not a very complicated process and the rewards can be tremendous.

HOW DOES AN ANNUITY PROTECT MY ASSETS?

The way an annuity has worked historically was, you put in a sum of money. Then, at a later date, the annuity would "annuitize," or, in other words, pay you a guaranteed income for a set number of years or a lifetime. The good news was the income was guaranteed. The bad news was that you no longer had access to your principal. This is how many pension plans work; you choose to take the lump sum or take the income.

In the past, annuities were offered many times by insurance companies and you had no control over the investment of your assets.

However, a properly structured annuity, created for your benefit, has tremendous advantages, including:

1. **All assets inside the annuity umbrella grow tax-deferred.** This is a big consideration for people who switch mutual funds often and pay capital gains, for people who continually rollover CDs and pay the tax on income every year, and for

the people who invested in tax-free bonds and bond funds but do not need the income.

2. **All income deferred inside the annuity is not figured into your gross income** at the end of the year, and your 1099 tax statement will show no income. The benefit is, your income will not be increased by the amount made inside the annuity, thus helping you stay below the income limitation on the taxation of your Social Security. Remember, although municipal bond interest is tax-free, it is still included in gross income for Social Security purposes.

3. **You do not have to give up access** to your income or principal while you are healthy.

4. **You can create these annuities in a favorable way** to choose where you want the investments directed. You can select mutual funds, government bond pools, or CD-type, insured accounts.

5. **You can use the annuity to create an exempt asset** for Medicaid purposes if implemented correctly. Meaning, you could keep your money, yet qualify for Medicaid.

Remember that creating an annuity and transferring your assets into it will not make the assets exempt. *If it is exempt at all, it is how the annuity is structured.*

Certain rules and guidelines for exempting assets and protecting assets must be followed. If you are using an annuity, you must create one with all the proper provisions and wording. If you use a prototype annuity, be sure they allow you to put in the provisions as needed.

Usually you can create the annuity and place both spouses' names on the contract. Then make one of your children the beneficiary. Assume you create this annuity and choose mutual funds in which to invest inside the annuity. You carry on as normal; switching funds, taking income or re-investing. If one spouse dies, the funds will not go through probate, the surviving spouse can keep the account active, or liquidate and take the funds, basically carrying on as normal. Note that once an annuity is created, it is very similar to an IRA. If you withdraw prior to 59 1/2 years of age you will have to pay penalties. And some annuities have penalties in addition to that.

Assume you are considering applying for Medicaid and one spouse gets sick. It is as this point that you invoke the provisions already established when you created your personal annuity.

First, the one transfer of assets that is allowed without disqualification under the 30-month look-back rule, is spousal transfer. So immediately make sure the annuity is in the healthy spouse's name. In addition, the beneficiary must not be the sick spouse. So change the beneficiary to either a separate trust or other beneficiaries.

Next, you must invoke certain provisions that should have already been established when you created your annuity. You must begin a periodic payment stream of both principal and interest for a set number of years. Compute what the least amount of income and principal is that you can take to remain below the income limitations for Medicaid. Since you have created your own annuity, you can dictate any provisions you want, so instruct the annuity to pay you, for example, nine dollars of interest per month and one dollar of principal. My point is that you do not have to pay yourself all that it earns because you want to lower your income when applying for Medicaid. This is truly where the loophole can be found. I don't think Medicaid anticipated that seniors would create their own personal annuities with the ability of implementing these provisions.

Some annuity companies will not pay whatever interest or principal you want. Many, especially if you do annuitize, will base the payoff on mortality tables depending on your age, the annuitant's age, and how long you want to receive the income. Obviously the longer you go, the lower the income will be, which is what you want when trying to protect money. Even if you go for the longest payout option and get the lowest interest rate, many companies will allow you to change your mind (called the ***Bail Out Provision***), after a certain number of years, usually five. The bail out provision will allow you to withdraw whatever is left of your account.

What the above sounds like you did is "annuitize your annuity." And for Medicaid purposes you did. It is paying period payments of principal and interest, you have no access to principal (while on Medicaid), and it has a set number of years for payments. The major difference is that you created this and implemented provisions that after a period of years (let's say five years), the income and principal payments stop, the cash becomes available again and is paid to either the healthy spouse or the beneficiaries. You might have to annuitize. You have to find a custodian who will allow it.

It is true that you do have to forgo access to principal while one of you is sick for a set number of years, but it sure beats spending all your money to pay the cost of a nursing home.

Note: This strategy is very complex and should be thoroughly discussed with an expert in the area. The discussion set forth is simply an introduction and no action should be taken by the information herein. And there is no guarantee these strategies will work.

HOW DOES THIS STRATEGY AFFECT MY INVESTMENTS?

As previously discussed, many insured money markets and popular mutual funds can be placed in your own personal variable annuity. You should be very clear that the custodian of the funds is secure and you understand all the provisions.

WHAT ARE THE COSTS?

If you understand investments, you can implement it by yourself and make a good selection without a broker commission or load. Some have maintenance charges or early withdrawal fees. Some have no fees and work very similar to a CD. It all depends on what you are trying to accomplish.

As for the fees to set it up, you should absolutely have an expert either in Elder Care Law, or Medicaid planning. Ask for the expert's credentials and references. I have heard of experts charging over $1,000 for this service, or include it as part of a larger, complete estate plan, or living trust package.

BE CAREFUL!

Make sure you understand all the good and bad points. Also, understand that laws can change at any time causing loopholes to close. Whoever creates this plan for you should use the highest quality custodians, making sure that some type of insurance from a very reputable carrier backs up the deposit.

ADDITIONAL CONSIDERATIONS

30-MONTH LOOK-BACK RULE

One of the Medicaid rules is the ***30-Month Look-Back Rule.*** The rule allows Medicaid to look back on financial dealings over the last 30 months. If Medicaid feels you made a transaction of gifting or giving money away, the money can be taken back. This is why you cannot gift large sums of an estate to a family member within 30 months of entering a nursing home. But it doesn't stop spousal transfers or buying a new home.

LAST OPTION - DIVORCE

You have heard tragedies about couples divorcing to protect from Medicaid. It's sad, but true. Everything gets transferred to one spouse and then the couple divorces in order to protected an estate. I am not going to even suggest anyone you use this tactic, or tell you it will always work. I mention it because people who have exhausted all other means have used this tactic.

MEDICAID PLANNING FOR AN UNMARRIED PERSON OR WIDOW(ER)

Unfortunately, planning for a single individual is much harder for several reasons, usually because you cannot take advantage of spousal transfers, the home might not be protected and the income allowance for single people is almost non-existent.

The reason a home is a protected asset is because one spouse (or tenant) is living in the home. However, if there is not other tenant in the home, the house would usually not be a protected asset.

To get around this problem, these popular tactics are often used:

1.   **LETTER OF INTENT.** You can still protect the home with a doctor's help. If you can get a doctor to sign a ***Letter of Intent,*** stating that your stay in a nursing home is temporary and you should be able to move back to the home in a short time (usually six months), then the house would be protected.

2.   **THE SECOND OPTION** is to place the house in joint tenancy usually with a child, and show that child living in the house with you. Of course, do this only if someone else is living with you and you feel comfortable placing their name on the title with you. Be careful of going higher than the free $10,000 gift per year or you might have to pay gift taxes or might have to use your one-time $600,000 exclusion. Also, once the property is placed in joint tenancy you lose half of the control. If you place someone on the deed who is married, you could actually be placing two people on your property (depending on the state in which you live).

3.   **THE THIRD OPTION** would be to create a life estate with the house. Basically, the parent signs the deed over to the children (or other beneficiaries), and as long as the parent is living, the children have no rights or access to the home. Upon the death of the parent, the home would go to the child. Then, if you were to apply for Medicaid, your home is protected since, technically, it is not yours. Upon death, Medicaid cannot place a lien on the property because the home is not owned by you.

4.   **THE FOURTH OPTION** would be to again consider annuities. The income limitation is very low for single individuals. But, a properly structured annuity can work very well. Invoke all the provisions discussed earlier but make someone else the annuitant. By nominating someone else the annuitant, you are allowing them to be the recipient of all the income, thus ensuring that your income will not be increased. You will also have to nominate someone else as the beneficiary. You lose control of the principal while you are on Medicaid for a set number of years but it is better to keep your money and lose a bit of control, than to waste all your hard-earned money on health care.

PART FOUR

WHERE TO INVEST
YOUR MONEY

CHAPTER 16

Types of Investments

There are probably more places to invest money than you can fathom. The important thing is understanding what is best for you, not your neighbor or another family member. What is right for you?

You won't be able to decide where to invest until you are comfortable with the *how to* invest. Literally, it is possible to spend your whole life learning about investments, reading books and educating yourself and still be unsure about your selections. In fact, most investors are unsure.

These next few chapters are specifically designed to give you a handle on making financial decisions for yourself, or at least give you enough knowledge to know what questions to ask.

The first rule of investing is: If, when your head hits the pillow at night, you are thinking about your investments, you are probably involved in the wrong investments. In determining where to invest, you can separate your decision into two categories of thought, *emotional and technical.*

KEEP IT TECHNICAL

If you can remove your emotions from your investment decisions and invest based only on the fundamental and technical reasons (logic, numbers, historical data, economy, industry and your financial plan), then you have a much greater chance of success. If you can't remove your emotions when making an investment decision, just don't invest. If investing makes you nervous, likewise, don't invest. If it means losing purchasing power by placing your money in a checking account at the bank, that's okay. If that makes you feel better, by all means keep it there. As they say, "It's the quality of life -- not the quantity that matters."

Remember you can lose money in an investment **and** you can lose money to inflation. Both are hazardous to your retirement. Inflation is one of the biggest destroyers of a happy retirement.

Although infinite types of investments exist for the mature American, one can successfully narrow down investment possibilities to a few major categories.

THE BANK

This is an institution that insures your deposits up to $100,000. The insurance is a corporation, backed by the government, and is called the ***Federal Deposit Insurance Corp. (FDIC).*** Although not actually part of the government, the government has pledged 100% backing. This means if your bank fails, the FDIC will pay you lost principal up to the amount of $100,000.

THE FDIC

Is it important to clearly understand the role of the FDIC. The first thing to realize is that you are only insured for a total of $100,000 of all the accounts in your name at any one bank.

In addition, if you open up similar accounts at two different branches of the same bank, you are only insured for the $100,000 total. This means if you have a $100,000 balance in the branch "A" checking account and $100,000 at branch "B" you are only insured for a total of $100,000.

Having several joint accounts will not get you around this law. Some investors try to get additional coverage by changing the order of the names on the accounts or the Social Security numbers. This will not work; the FDIC considers these all the same account.

In addition, any account held in trust for someone else (Note: I am not referring to a living trust, but a trust account) is still an account considered to be in your name. Instead, you must open an account for someone the FDIC defines as "a natural object of your bounty," which is a child, grandchild or spouse. These accounts are considered separate from each other and each are insured for up to $100,000.

If you have IRA, SEP and KEOGH accounts at any one bank, these are also included in the total of $100,000 per institution. However, current legislation is considering *Grandfathering* those accounts established prior to December 19, 1992, to allow each account to have up to $100,000 of coverage.

WHAT BANKS OFFER

Once you have selected a bank, you can usually choose a passbook savings account, checking account, or a common *Certificate of Deposit (CD).* Usually the owner of a CD will enjoy a better interest rate for allowing the bank to tie up their money for a period of time.

Many banks offer brokerage services right in the branch. These brokerages often sell government and growth mutual funds, stocks, bonds, and annuities. Although this service is not a bad one, make no mistake about how they work. These in-house bank "investment counselors" usually work for a separate department within the bank. Usually, your investments are not guaranteed by FDIC and are not deposited in your bank. The counselors usually earn a separate commission for your investments, so be sure in advance how that commission works. Know all the risks, fees and caveats. Read the prospectus as if you are investing in a company outside the bank.

The strongest feature of a bank is the insurance from potential loss of your principal. Other advantages of the bank might include the ease of depositing and withdrawing your money, using automated cash machines, transmitting funds and many convenient or free services.

The downside of using a bank is that you pay an awfully big price for those advantages. In today's economic environment, the bank's interest rates are so low that, after inflation and taxes, you actually lose purchasing power. This is a critical fact for mature Americans to know.

BONDS

Historically, bonds have been a terrific source for higher income with relative security of your principal. Bonds are usually considered safer than a stock or equity position because you are lending money to a company, government or municipality (risk is determined by the type of bond). If a bond issue goes broke, usually the bondholder will be paid before an equity investor in the case of a bankruptcy proceeding.

Simply stated, a bond means that you, the investor, are lending money to an entity at a specified interest rate for a specified time. Bonds are usually offered in denominations of $100 or $1,000. A typical bond would work like this: you lend $1,000 to an entity (for example, the United States government). In return, they promise to pay you 8% (or $80) per year until the bond matures. The bond is stated to mature in ten years so at the end of ten years you receive your $1,000 back.

Your guarantee in any bond represents the entity or the insurance company backing it. The bond in the above case is U.S. government-issued and they will back the bond. Most investors would agree that this is very safe.

Remember, it is not the bond itself that is safe or risky. A bond is just a type of security. The risk of the bond depends on the type of bond you buy. You might read a headline in the paper stating, "Bond prices are going down." Don't let a statement like that influence your decision. There are so many bonds and so many differences between bonds, not to mention how people use them, that bond headlines might not even pertain to your situation at all.

8% (PERCENTAGE RATE)

DUE 2017 (YEAR OF MATURITY)

(NAME OF COMPANY)

REGISTERED

WESTERN BELL TELEPHONE AND TELEGRAPH COMPANY

REGISTERED

FORTY YEAR 8% DEBENTURE, DUE MAY 1, 2017
(TERM, PERCENTAGE , DUE DATE)

Western Bell Telelphone and Telegraph Company, a California corporation herein referred to as the Company, promises to payee...

(BOND NUMBER)	(BOND HOLDER)	(NUMBER OF BONDS)
RU 087401	KENNETH A. STERN	23000***
DW 7215171		*23000**
		**23000*
		***23000
	***TWENTY THREE THOUSAND ***	

(LEGAL DESCRIPTION)

Ldithdl ldisioc sldide dldldls eididl sldkfu sldiui ald ldioao dliei fldaof lddf idie di idajdfk ldkjke diaoi kdalkfj kdjfalkj ifdiei dkciciel ldkfjafj idfuiejgjkcm oifiao eiudl kdithdl ldisioc sldide dldldls eididl sldkfu sldiui ald ldioao dliei fldaof lddf idie di ii idajdfk ldkjke diaoi kdalkfj kdjfalkj ifdiei dkciiciel ldkfjafj idfuiejgjkcm oifiao eiudlkdithdl ldisioc sldide dldldls eididl sldkfu sldiui ald ldioao dliei fldaof lddf idie di idajdfk ldkjke diaoi kdalkfj kdjfalkj ifdiei dkciiciel ldkfjafj idfuiejgjkcm oifiao eiudl kdithdl ldisioc sldide dldldls eididl sldkfu sldiui ald ldioao dliei fldaof lddf idie di i idajdfk ldkjke diaoi kdalkfj kdjfalkj ifdiei dkciiciel ldkfjafj idfuiejgjkcm oifiao eiudl kdithdl ldisioc sldide dldldls eididl sldkfu sldiui ald ldioao dliei fldaof lddf idie di i idajdfk ldkjke diaoi kdalkfj kdjfalkj ifdiei dkciiciel ldkfjfj idfuiejgjkcm oifiao eiud kdithdl ldisioc sldide dldldls eididl sldkfu sldiui ald ldioao dliei fldaof lddf idie di i id...

Witness Whereof...Western Bell Telephone amd Telegraph Company has caused this investment be signed by its President, Treasurer and Assistant Treasurer, each by a facsimile of his signature, and has caused a facsimileof its corporate seal to be...

03/13/92

**(DATE OF
PURCHASE)**

CERTIFICATE OF AUTHENTICATION
This is one of the Debentures desribed
in the within mentioned indenture
NORTH CAROLINA NATIONAL BANK
As Trustee
Authenticating Agency

**ALTERNATE CERTIFICATE OF
AUTHENTICATION**
This is one of the debenture described
in the within mentioned indenture
Authenticating Agency
As Trustee
BY THE CHASEMANHATTAN BANK
(NATIONAL ASSOCIATION)

By **(SIGNATURE OF OFFICER)**

AGENCIES FOR TRANSFER, EXCHANGE AND PAYMENT: NORTH CAROLINA NATIONAL BANK (CHARLOTTE, N.C.) AND THE CHASE MANHATTAN BANK

(TRANSFER AGENT)

It is relatively easy to track a bond to determine its safety. Since this should be a major criterion when choosing a bond, it is worth doing this investigative work. First, you can go to the library and research the bond rating. The major rating services are *Standard and Poor's* or *Moody's.* Usually you can review the rating of that particular bond (from AAA to CCC). The rating services will also tell you about the bond offering along with their opinion of it. To arrive at a rating many factors are considered, including the debt structure, financial statements and solvency. They are rated as follows:

MOODY'S		S&P
AAA	Highest quality	AAA
AA	High quality	AA
A	Good quality	A
BAA	Medium quality with some speculative qualities	BBB
BA	Speculative but with some defensive qualities	BBB
B	Highly speculative	CCC
	Bonds that stated interest is not	
CAA	being paid or those in default	CC
C	Lowest rating	D

In addition, within each category, these rating companies might add a (+) or (-) to be more exact on the pricing.

BOND INSURANCE

Many times you see an advertisement for an *AAA-Rated Insured Bond.* It is extremely important to know who is insuring your bond. Is the bond issued by the U.S. government or one of its direct agencies (such as a *Ginnie Mae)*? This implied backing is the full faith and credit of the U.S. government and is considered AAA-rated and insured by the government.

However, if I issue a bond to raise money to market this book, I might say, "This bond is insured," but by what? What if the assets of my corporation don't even equal the amount raised by my bond offering? Often, issuers of municipal or corporate bonds will "insure" their bonds in order to receive an AAA rating. If a bond has a good insurance rating, chances are Standard and Poor's or Moody's will raise the rating of the bond.

Still, be sure to ask who is insuring the bond. Usually a bond is insured in the same way you buy life insurance. Bond issuers go to an insurance company that specializes in insuring bonds and pays for the insurance. If the bond defaults, typically the insurance on the bond will guarantee bondholders their money back. What you need to decide is if the company that is insuring the bond is a strong, solvent company.

Usually the insurance companies that are used for bond issues are large, publicly-held companies. As a result, you can research the company by using various techniques. Many of the techniques are the same used to evaluate a stock. You can go to the library or call the company and ask for an annual report. Or you can review a value line on the company. During the 1990s some insurance companies that reinsured municipal bonds failed, so be careful.

TYPES OF BONDS

SAVINGS BONDS

In recent years, Series EE United States Government savings bonds have regained their popularity. You can buy these bonds for half their value at maturity. And they are backed by the full faith and credit of the U.S. government. They do not pay current interest, however, and the tax on the accrued earnings is deferred until you cash the bond.

Of course, sooner or later the tax must be paid. What some investors do is convert these savings bonds, upon their maturity, into HH bonds. By converting to HH bonds you can avoid the big tax bite. However, HH bonds do pay current interest on which you are taxed. Usually the HH bond does not enjoy as high an interest rate as EE bonds.

If you don't want or don't need current income, EE bonds might be a wise alternative to another secure "safe money" investment.

UNITED STATES TREASURY BILLS, NOTES AND BONDS

The biggest difference between a bill and a bond is the maturity. A treasury bill usually matures at 30, 60, or 90 day intervals. A note has a maturity usually over one year, but less then ten years. A treasury bond can mature anywhere from 10-30 years.

The other major difference is how the interest is paid. A Treasury Bill is issued at a discount. Instead of paying $1,000 for a bond you might pay $800 for a bill. When the bill matures you will receive the full $1,000. A Treasury Bond is issued for the full face value of $1,000 and will pay you at the current interest rate (usually semi-annually). United States Treasury obligations are free from all state tax.

TAX-FREE BONDS

A tax-free bond is usually a bond issued by a municipality – a school district, city or state. If you buy a tax-free municipal bond in the state where you live, it will usually be free of any tax on the interest paid both on a federal and state level. If you buy a tax-free municipal bond in a state that is not your principal residence, it is usually free from all federal taxes, but you will pay your state tax.

Just because a bond is tax free does not mean it is safe. A bond could be tax free and issued against a hospital in the state where you live. If that hospital fails, the bond could default and you can lose your money. Always check to see if the bond you are buying is insured and by whom. Also, be sure you agree with the purpose of the bond.

In a broad sense, two major types of municipal bonds exist – *General Obligation Bonds and Revenue Bonds.* When purchasing a bond, it is important to be able to distinguish the difference.

General Obligation Bonds are usually obligations issued directly by a municipality and backed by that municipality. For example, if the State of California issues a General Obligation Bond, the chances are that it is backed by the full faith and credit of the State of California. In the past, this would have (and still might be) considered to be very safe and secure. However, more and more people are concerned about the health and credit quality of certain states.

Revenue Bonds are backed by the revenue a particular bond is offering to generate. For example, if you purchase a bond for the Buffalo County School District, your bond is directed toward the financing of a school district. If the school district fails, so will your bond. Although this bond is still double tax free and a municipal bond, the State of New York has no obligation to back these bonds or bail them out if the project fails. In essence, revenue bonds carry a higher degree of risk than general obligation bonds. To account for that, and to get revenue bonds an AAA-rating, you will often see these bonds backed by private insurers that guarantee your principal.

Be careful when investing in municipal bonds. There is more confusion and more poor investment decisions in this category than with any other asset. Many people think their investments are insured and safe when actually, they are not. In fact, many municipal bonds are considered "junk bonds" or not credit-worthy.

CORPORATE BONDS

The same concept applies when you are lending a corporation money. In other words, you are the bank. In return, you will receive a specific interest rate and the return of your money upon maturity. There are corporations that are considered extremely safe and some that are a bit more risky. The more risk you take the higher the return (interest rate).

In the past, bonds that were not rated BB or above have been termed "junk" bonds. However, for the person who knows how to evaluate a company and who understands how to determine the level of risk, higher returns can be achieved. Remember, since you are a bond holder, your investment is different than owning stock. The bondholder gets paid the interest first, before the shareholder receives dividends in every case – including bankruptcy.

Before purchasing a corporate bond, ask several questions. Research the company to determine how much debt the company carries. If the company has a high debt/asset ratio (like 80%), how do they plan to reduce it? Check to see if the profitability of the company is increasing. And see if they have ever missed an interest payment or have defaulted on an interest payment.

GINNIE MAE, FANNIE MAE, FREDDIE MAC

These funds include all types of securities issued by agencies of the government. Although not actually guaranteed by the full faith and credit of the United States government, they are assumed to carry the same implied credit. A *Ginnie Mae* has the highest safety level because it is an actual part of the government and has an AAA rating.

You must be careful when investing in these securities since it is much harder to evaluate your investment. The attractive points include a better interest rate than a government bond, different maturities and the safety of the government agency backing it up. However, the maturity dates are not definite. Most of these securities are backed by pools of mortgages. If mortgage rates are lowered and many Americans refinance their home mortgages, your Ginnie Mae certificate could pay off early. Or, as sometimes happens, chunks of your principal will come back to you over a period of years.

If that is the case, you will need to reinvest your money sooner than expected. The interest and principal is paid back many times on the same check. You must be careful to reinvest the principal and only use the income from the Ginnie Mae. When the certificate is completely paid, you will have already received all of your interest and principal back. Nothing will be left. If you hold the certificate with a brokerage company, you might even consider asking them to hold the principal payments and send you only the interest.

ZERO COUPON BONDS

An interesting twist to investment in bonds has been the use of *Zero Coupon Bonds*. A zero coupon bond does not pay interest. Instead of paying $1,000 per bond you can buy it for a discount at perhaps $500 (like a Series EE savings bond). The discount depends on maturity and the rating. When the bond matures you will receive the full $1,000 per bond.

Many people think the only zero coupon bonds are zero coupon treasury bonds, but this is not true. If your broker suggests you buy a zero coupon bond, make sure you know the issuer – whether it is the government, a corporation or another entity. Some investors question if it makes sense to buy a bond that does not pay interest. Why buy it at a discount and wait for it to mature to face value? Isn't that what a U.S. Savings Bond (Series EE) does?

The reason that most people reject current interest is because the bond pays a higher interest rate than if you were receiving immediate, steady interest. Other investors like to use this method knowing that a certain amount of money will be available on a particular date. For instance, one might use this to fund a grandchild's education.

Although you are not receiving current interest, on a zero coupon bond, you still have to report the taxable income every year, that is, unless it is a tax-free zero coupon.

INTEREST RATES AND PRICES
WHEN BUYING A BOND

The average retiree's investment portfolio usually consists heavily of bonds – either through government mutual funds, income funds, or straight bonds. As good as bonds might look, they still have disadvantages. Remember, when buying a bond, to be careful of the interest rate and the price of the bond.

If you buy a bond with a stated interest rate of 8% and you pay $1,200 for each bond, you have paid a $200 premium. In other words, you paid $200 more per bond than what the issuer will give you back when the bond matures. You will only receive $1,000 back. This, of course, lowers what is termed the *Yield to Maturity*. Yes, you will still get the 8% interest, but since you do not get your $1,200 back, thus the actual yield you earned was only about 6% (depending on the bond maturity). Unless the bond is a truly terrific deal (high yield to maturity), be careful of paying too much more than $1,000 per bond. In fact, try to pay under $1,000 per bond (at a discount).

I am sure you have heard it said that investors buy at all the wrong times. Unfortunately, when the greed factor comes into play, this is sometimes true. For example, from 1990 to 1992, interest rates plummeted. If, at the end of that period, you could buy a AAA-rated bond paying 8% would you? If you said yes, you answered too quickly. I may have told you the bond is AAA rated, but I did not tell you the maturity. Those bonds were available at the end of 1992. The maturity dates on these bonds were about 30 years. Many investors bought these bonds and they may prove to be a very wise investment. Only time will tell, depending on interest rates.

If interest rates rise, the price of your bond will decrease. Conversely, if interest rates continue to trend down, your bond price will go up – until maturity.

If you own an individual bond, like a U.S. government bond, and you have every intention of holding it to maturity, then you should not care about the daily market price of your bond or the fact that other bonds might be paying higher interest. You might read that bond prices are down and you may want to sell your bond, or that interest rates are going up and your bond will lose value. *Why care what the price is today if you hold it until maturity? You shouldn't because you are guaranteed your $1,000 per bond back.*

But if interest rates rise and you need to sell your bond before maturity, no one will give you $1,000 per bond. Why should they? If you bought a U.S. government bond yielding 8% and two years later the same U.S. government bond is yielding 9%, who would buy your old bond when the new one is paying 9%? In order to sell the bond you will have to sell it at a discount. Instead of selling the bond for the price you paid of $1,000, you might have to sell it for $900. This is what is meant by the axiom, "When interest rates rise, bond prices go down."

It is important to remember that if you have already determined in your financial plan that your required return is 8%, your job should be to invest in as many 8% AAA-rated vehicles as possible. If your required return is truly only 8%, you do not have to worry about recessions, interest rates or inflation. You have correctly completed your financial plan and know that in order to live comfortably for the rest of your life, all you need is an 8% return.

However, trouble comes when you enter retirement based on the fact that you will be earning about 8% and then you are able to earn only 4%. Even worse, it may turn out that the 4% inflation rate you counted on has risen to 6%. Believe me, you are going to run out of money a lot sooner than you anticipated.

Perhaps one of the biggest risks associated with a bond, aside from the credibility or solvency of the issuer, is the interest rate. *It is said that bonds are the greatest investment during periods of deflation, but during periods of high inflation, bonds will lose value.* It is similar to the previous example – if you buy a bond paying 8% today and next year the same bond is being offered at 9%, you will not be able to sell your bond to buy the 9% bond without losing some money. If inflation rates rise dramatically and you buy 5% yielding bonds and inflation is at 6%, you are losing money to the tune of 1% per year. Based on your increasing life span, it is possible, if you are not mindful and careful, to outlive your money!

This book is attempting to tell you is something you probably already know – that *everything runs in cycles.* If you are retiring during a period of low inflation, don't discount its potency. Inflation will rear its ugly head and, if you are not properly prepared, inflation can devastate your life. It is an ironic fact that many people think it is truly great having banks pay interest of over 10% however, with inflation at 12%, you are losing more than you were earning. Sound familiar?

Although there are many other types of bonds, the ones mentioned above are the most common. Some people invest in a straight bond, while others invest in bond mutual funds or trusts. Again, it all depends on your particular needs.

HOW TO PURCHASE BONDS

Although there are many additional types of bonds, those discussed above are among the most common. Some investors buy a straight bond, while others invest in bond mutual funds or trusts. It will depend on your particular needs.

Usually you purchase a bond through a broker. You may either purchase a new bond, or an existing bond in the after-market. The broker will probably add one or two percentage points to the price of the bond (the wholesale price) and sell it to you with his commission included. This is the retail price. Be sure to ask the amount of the commission. Some companies will issue bonds directly to an investor. You can call shareholder services of that company to find out.

STOCKS

A *Stock* is simply an equity ownership in a corporation. If you own a share of McDonalds, you are, in fact, a part owner of the corporation. Although many kinds of stocks exist such as preferred or common, the basic premise is that you are a part owner of the company. If the company does well, so will your stock. If the company does poorly, the stock will probably also do poorly.

The prices of stocks vary from pennies per share to over $1,000 per share. This means, if the price per share is $10 and you buy 100 shares, you will spend $1,000. The alluring aspect of a stock is that the price per share fluctuates. If the price of that $10 share goes to $11 per share, you just made 10% on your investment. That could happen in as little time as an hour, a day, a week, or a year. Unfortunately the stock could go to $9 or less per share just as easily.

There are many kinds of companies in which you can buy stock. Small companies that are new usually start at a low share price. Obviously the risk is greater. These stocks are referred to as *"Small Cap"* stocks. *"Mid-Cap"* stocks consist of middle-sized companies. The larger companies are considered much safer and are sometimes called *"Blue-Chip"* stocks.

THE STOCK MARKET

Many people refer to the stock market as, simply, *the market* but it is important to consider which market they are talking about or if they are talking about a particular index. Several companies are responsible for tracking the performance of stocks through indices. The most well-known include:

THE DOW JONES INDUSTRIAL AVERAGE

Perhaps the most popular index, the **Dow Jones Average**, measures 30 large industrial stocks. Arguably you might ask, how can this be a true measure of the stock market considering thousands of companies trade stock? Many professionals agree, thus the reason for different indices in which to track your area of interest. Each of the 30 stocks in the Dow are weighted differently according to price and size of the company and its stock.

STANDARD AND POOR'S 500

The Standard and Poor's 500 is a broad index which typically includes the 500 leading stocks. There are many other indices of this type including the Standard and Poor's 100, specialty utility indices, bio-tech and others.

NEW YORK STOCK EXCHANGE

The New York Stock Exchange is both a market where stocks are traded and an index. All stocks that trade on the NYSE make up this index.

TRADING STOCK

Many different methods and exchanges exist for trading stock. The name **Wall Street** has often symbolized the stock market. For many years the NYSE on Wall Street was the largest and most prestigious exchange "auction" in which to trade your stock. This exchange is an actual physical location where people meet, in an auction setting, to trade stock.

Gaining greater popularity is an **Over-the-Counter** exchange sometimes referred to as NASDAQ, or the National Association of Securities Dealers Automated Quotation System. If I were to ask you, "Where is the stock market?" you might answer, "New York." But that is only the New York Stock Exchange. If I were to ask, "Where is the over-the-counter market?" you could not answer because there is no physical location. Buys and sells on the NASDAQ are instantly matched by a computer and executed without anyone ever having to go into a pit or special arena to trade.

Historically, the smaller companies listed securities on the over-the-counter exchange, since it was easier for these companies to be accepted for listing. Thus the popularity of the NASDAQ as an index for smaller cap stocks was established. Although it is still very difficult to list with the NYSE, usually the larger companies trade on it. However, the NASDAQ is gaining popularity with larger companies as well.

WHERE AND HOW DO STOCKS GET PURCHASED?

A stock can be purchased sometimes by directly calling the company and asking for the Shareholder Services Department or by calling a stockbroker. If you are just learning how to buy stocks, there is wisdom in calling a broker or a financial planner since he or she may be better prepared to offer you some good direction or advice.

Many people ask, "Who determines the price of a stock?" The answer is, "You and I do." It's supply and demand. If I think a company is going to do financially well, I can call a broker and ask him or her to buy the stock at the current price. At that point I own the stock. I do not have to sell my stock until someone pays me the price I want, whatever that may be. If someone buys my shares at my asking price, the new value, or new price of the stock, is established.

You have a choice of having a certificate for the shares you buy, or keeping it at the company or the brokerage firm. The benefit of keeping the certificate at the firm is that the they are insured and liable for the certificate. Don't worry about there being a record of you owning the stock because you will receive periodic statements along with other information from either the company directly or the brokerage house where the shares were purchased. If you ask to keep the shares, you will be responsible for their safekeeping.

WHICH TYPE OF STOCK SHOULD BE BOUGHT?

Generally there are two types of stocks – preferred and common. *Preferred Stocks* are in a preferred position to common stock because preferred shareholders are paid dividends first. If a company goes bankrupt, for example, the proceeds from the bankruptcy would first go to pay the *preferred* shareholders before the *common* shareholders. As a result, the price of the preferred stock is usually less volatile. Many people buy preferred stock to obtain a higher yield with greater stability of principal. Some stocks, mostly preferred, pay a steady dividend, much like a bond. The investor also has the chance of having the stock increase in value as the company's profits increase. However, if the company does poorly, your share price could go down. But, for the higher risk, you probably will enjoy a better *Dividend* or interest rate, on your money.

If you are good at picking a strong, solid company and need additional income, a preferred stock could be an excellent source of steady income with an opportunity for growth of your investment.

A **Common Stock** is generally just an equity, or ownership, position with a company. As this type of stock involves more risk, the share price will fluctuate more. Common stockholders usually have voting privileges, whereas only some preferred issues offer voting privileges. The voting privileges allow the investor to vote in an election of the company's board of directors and other important issues.

HOW TO WATCH THE PRICE OF THE STOCK

There are many ways you can watch how your stock is performing. Your broker can give you the current price, you can call Shareholder Services at the company where you are investing, or you can look in the financial section of the newspaper.

READING THE STOCK PAGE

Common stock traded on the New York Stock Exchange (NYSE) or the American Stock Exchange (AMEX) are listed in the financial press in the following manner:

52-Week High	Low	Stock	Div	Yield %	P/E Ratio	Sales 100s	High	Low	Close	Net Change
36 3/8	25 3/8	ABC	1.16	3.7	9	60	32	31 3.8	31 3.8	+ 1/8
47 1/2	28 1/4	DEF	.80	1.9	23	6	42	42	42	---
37 7/8	18	XYZ	.40	1.3	11	1	30 7/8	30 1/2	30 7/8	-1/4

Reading from left to right, the columns are interpreted as follows:

52 Week **High Low**	This column lists the highest and lowest price at which the stock sold per share in the past 52 weeks. For example, the year's high for ABC is 36 3/8, or $36.375, whereas the year's low is 25 3/8, or $25.375. The year's high for DEF is 47 1/2, or $47.50, whereas the year's low is 28 1/4, or $28.25.
Stock	This column lists the abbreviated name of the stock being reported.
Div	This column lists the annual cash dividend per share of stock based on the rate of the last quarterly payout. The dividend per share of ABC stock is $1.16. For DEF stock, the dividend per share is $.80; and for XYZ, the annual dividend is $.40.

Yield %	This column represents the dividend yield, which is found by dividing the dollar amount of the dividend by the closing price of the stock. The result is then multiplied by 100 to produce the actual yield percentage. Dividend yield is a measure of the flow of income produced by an investment in a particular stock. The dividend yields for ABC, DEF, and XYZ are 3.7%, 1.9% and 1.3%, respectively.
P/E Ratio	This column lists the price-earnings ratio of the stock, or the ratio of the latest closing price of the stock to the latest available annual earnings per share of the firm. The P/E ratio for ABC indicates that the stock is selling for 9 times the company's earnings. Earnings per share can be calculated by dividing the closing price on the day being reported by the P/E ratio. For ABC, earnings per share are $3.49 ($31.375/9).
Sales	This data represents the volume of transactions (shares) bought and sold on the trading day considered. The entry is presented in the hundreds; that is, the entry must be multiplied by 100 to arrive at the actual volume of transactions. The number of shares traded for ABC, DEF, and XYZ are 6000, 600 and 100, respectively.
High	This entry represents the highest selling price of one share of stock for the day considered. The highest selling prices for ABC, DEF, and XYZ on the trading day considered are $32, $42 and $30.875, respectively.
Low	This entry represents the lowest selling price of one share of stock for the day considered. The lowest selling prices for ABC, DEF, and XYZ are $31.375, $42, and $30.875, respectively.
Close	This column lists the price of the last share of stock sold on the day considered. The prices of the last share sold for ABC, DEF, and XYZ are $31.375, $42, and $30.875, respectively.
Net Change	This column lists the net change between the closing price of the stock on the day considered and the closing price on the previous trading day. A plus sign preceding the number indicates that the closing price for the day considered is higher than for the previous day, whereas a minus sign indicates that the closing price is less than for the previous day. The net change for ABC is +1/8, which indicates that the closing price for the previous day was 31 1/4, or $31.25 per share. There is no net change for DEF; this indicates that the closing price from the previous day was 42, or $42 per share. The net change for XYZ is -1/4; this indicates that the closing prices on the previous trading day was 31 1/8, or $31.125 per share.

HOW TO PICK A STOCK

Before you invest, have your financial plan in place and know what you are trying to accomplish. Then you will know the type of stock you want to buy. Next, review the asset allocation of your portfolio and be very clear on what you need to do to fill the gaps that may exist in your investments. Like an artist creating a painting, you decide on the colors and where you need to make additions or changes.

There are many theories about how to buy stocks. Some theories concentrate on *Dividend Theory,* while others focus on *Price-To-Earnings Evaluation.* With so many ways to pick stocks, the important thing to remember is that none of them is foolproof. If there were a foolproof method, the market would compensate for it and it probably would not work any longer. Always be careful and don't invest your money if you can't tolerate market fluctuations and possible losses.

In a broad sense, the two approaches to picking a stock are the *fundamental* and *technical* approaches.

The fundamental approach entails watching the economy, market trends and how well a particular company is positioned to perform in the market place against its immediate competition and the industry as a whole.

The technical approach involves researching a particular company's balance sheet, income statements, cash flow, book value, price-to-earnings ratio and debt-to-equity ratio.

In my opinion, a prudent stock investor should utilize the best of both approaches.

A SIMPLE CHECK LIST IN THE EVALUATION OF A STOCK WOULD INCLUDE:

1.   FIND OUT IF THE BUSINESS OF A COMPANY IS GROWING.

And find out if their competition is heavy and increasing.

2.   EVALUATE THE PRICE-TO-EARNINGS RATIO.

This will test how expensive the stock is to buy. If you divide the most recent price by the earnings per share, you will get a *Price-to-Earnings (P/E) Ratio.* This tells you how many times the company's earnings the stock selling price may be. The higher the number, the more expensive the stock.

For instance, if the P/E ratio of a company is 10, the stock is selling at 10 times the earnings. Usually the large, blue chip stocks will trade at a higher P/E ratio because investors are willing to pay more for what they assume is a more safe investment. Basically you pay more for an implied, safe investment. Hopefully this type of company has a better chance of safe growth.

New companies, with lower P/E ratios, sometimes interest investors who think the stock will rise dramatically. Sometimes you might find a stock with a low P/E ratio and all the other stocks in that asset category are trading at higher P/E ratios. Research the company's history and find out if there is a reason why their P/E is lower. If you find no substantial reason, it might simply be that the analysts do not follow the stock and therefore offer no opinion, which could create demand. This could present a buying opportunity.

You might also want to look at the index into which you are thinking about buying take the average P/E ratio from that index. For example, if you buy into a DOW stock and the DOW stocks are averaging a 14% P/E, you might try to find one trading at a little less.

3.   WHAT ARE THE COMPANY'S EARNINGS?

Are the earnings rising every year and for how many years have they risen? It's an important factor as you make a judgment call. You can look at revenue or cash flow, which might be increasing every year. But if the earnings per share are not also increasing, why would it matter if the company is bringing in more money?

4.   WHAT IS THE DEBT STRUCTURE OF THE COMPANY?

How leveraged are they? If you own your home free and clear, there is little to no chance a bank could take away your house if earnings are bad one year. Conversely, if a company has borrowed a great deal of money and has a bad year, it might be in trouble when the bank comes to collect.

For most stocks the average mature American would be most likely to consider, a good rule of thumb would be to stay with low-to no-debt companies.

5.   KNOW THE STOCK DIVIDEND YIELD.

Also how many times that dividend has increased or decreased since the company's beginning? Often the price of the stock is supported by the dividend the company pays the investor. If the dividend is cut, or stopped, the stock could fall dramatically in price.

Many investors use the dividend theory to pick stocks. The theory: Stocks that have always increased their dividend and never decreased it over a period of time, will perform better than the market average. Furthermore, the stock will not fall as much as other stocks when the market is down. Some people refine this theory even further by adding more criteria, such as: the stock cannot be trading at over two or three times the book value; the P/E ratio must be 10% under the market average; or, earnings per share should be expected to increase next year.

These are just some examples of the criteria investors might use to pick stocks. For the mature American who enjoys owning stocks, the dividend theory seems to be a prudent way to invest. This theory might be more safe than the market average and, over time, have good potential for success. The easiest way to loosely practice the DOW dividend theory is to find the highest yielding stocks in the DOW that have the lowest prices.

6.   WHAT IS THE 200 DAY MOVING AVERAGE OF A STOCK?

If a stock has already risen well above the moving average, you must ask yourself, "Why is the stock rising? How much further can it go past its average?" Some investors actually like to buy the stock after it dips below its moving average. Why? Perhaps the market dipped for whatever reason and the stock you are tracking dropped as well, but for no apparent reason than a general market drop. This could be a buying opportunity.

7.   FIND OUT WHAT THE ANALYSTS SAY ABOUT THE STOCK.

Do they like it? Why? What do they think the earnings per share will do over the next few years?

8.   BASED ON THE ECONOMY TODAY, HOW WILL THIS COMPANY PERFORM FIVE OR TEN YEARS FROM NOW?

How would it do in a recession or expansion? Again, it all reverts back to what you are trying to accomplish with the stock. Most mature Americans should not be taking excessive risk. If they do like picking stocks, I believe it should be done correctly, which is conservatively and over a period of time. It's simply a matter of what criteria you use to pick the stock. The hot craze one year might be toy stocks, but during a recession toys are not a necessity. Along those same lines, think of industries that will always be in demand. Then pick a good, solid company in that arena.

9.   IS THE COMPANY ENVIRONMENTALLY FRIENDLY?
With the new administration, there is a consensus that major businesses will have to make many changes to help clean up the environment. Companies that have already done so will not have to bear such a large cost.

10.   WHAT IS THE MOMENTUM OF THE STOCK?
Are more investors and institutions buying the stock? Is this good, or is it artificially raising the stock price to higher levels than it should? Or, is the reverse true? Has there been some negative news that may have caused a selling frenzy at a lower price than where the stock should be trading?

11.   FINALLY, ARE YOU WILLING TO LOSE MONEY?
Regardless of all the research and studying you might do, a stock can still lose money. You must be aware of this and willing to take the risk.

The problem many investors have is that they don't buy or sell at the right time. Many investors buy too late, after a story on a particular company is already old. By then, this stock is be selling too high. The sophisticated investor has already sold, driving the price down and the poor investor who bought late panics and sells low. Guess who's starting to buy again? If you hear about a good stock story through a friend, it may be too late for you. Review the last ten points and if the stock still checks out, then consider it. Even then, only consider the investment as a potential if it fits in with your financial plan.

Find a good company whose stock you are willing to hold for a long time. If the stock market takes a dive, and your stock in particular, you must treat that as a bonus – a buying opportunity. Now you can invest in that same stock at a discount. Just because Wall Street is foolish does not mean you can't be savvy and enjoy a buying opportunity.

You also must be ready to sell. If your stock is getting expensive, don't be afraid to continue selling at certain intervals. You will know if it is getting expensive by reviewing the previous ten criteria. After your stock goes up 20%, if it is too expensive (if earnings are not up 20%), sell the gain. After 50%, if the stock is too expensive, consider selling the rest. Remember, don't sell if the stock is up 50% if the earnings are up as well, and don't fall in love emotionally with your stock, if the ratio goes up too high.

One of the best sources of stock tracking is *The Daily Graphs,* published by William O'Neil & Co., which includes a complete explanation on reading stock graphs.

EXAMPLE OF A STOCK

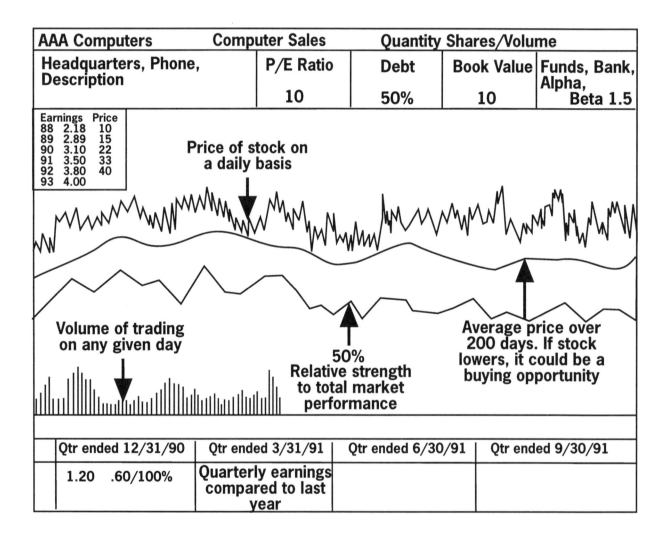

AAA Computers	Computer Sales	Quantity Shares/Volume		
Headquarters, Phone, Description	P/E Ratio	Debt	Book Value	Funds, Bank, Alpha, Beta 1.5
	10	50%	10	

Earnings	Price
88	2.18	10
89	2.89	15
90	3.10	22
91	3.50	33
92	3.80	40
93	4.00	

Price of stock on a daily basis

Volume of trading on any given day

50% Relative strength to total market performance

Average price over 200 days. If stock lowers, it could be a buying opportunity

Qtr ended 12/31/90	Qtr ended 3/31/91	Qtr ended 6/30/91	Qtr ended 9/30/91
1.20 .60/100%	Quarterly earnings compared to last year		

EXPLANATION OF STOCK TERMS

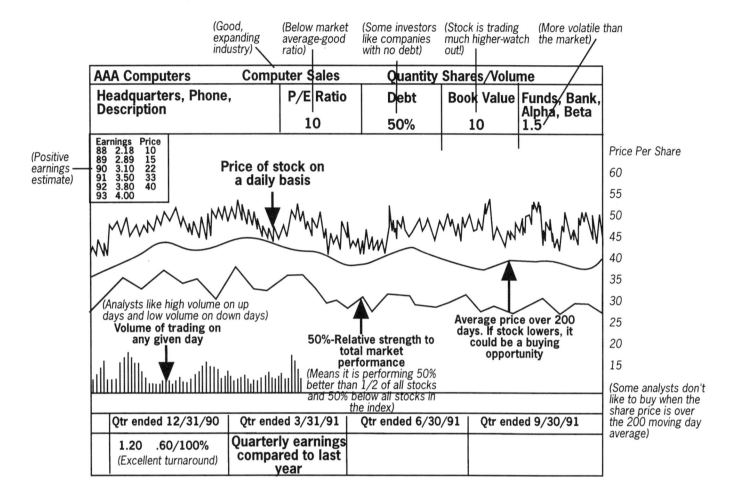

WHERE TO FIND STOCK INFORMATION

All the information we have discussed is readily available, and analysts use it every day. The following are easy suggestions for obtaining stock information:

1.   USE A BROKER

A broker gets paid a commission when you do trades, so make sure he or she earns the money. If he calls you recommending a stock, don't do your own research. Ask the broker to send you the answers to your ten questions.

A discount broker will not give you as much information. You simply call a discount broker and tell him or her what trade you wish to make. You have to do the research.

2. DO RESEARCH AT THE LIBRARY

The library usually subscribes to all of the publications that would have answers to your questions. *Value Line* is a publication that would answer most of the previous ten questions. The library might even have *The Daily Graphs* and the *Standard and Poor's Stock Guides,* which would help as well.

3. CALL THE COMPANY

The company's Shareholder Services Department should give you any financial information you request. You can even ask them who the *Market Maker* of their stock is and the phone number. The market maker is the person, or company, in charge of the whole stock underwriting. The market maker will send you any information you request.

4. OBTAIN PERIODICALS

You can obtain, if you want to spend the money, literally hundreds of periodicals pertaining to anything from simple stock picks to complex graphs and projections. But don't spend the money, just go to a public library and cross reference all newsletters and periodicals that contain stock selection criteria.

MUTUAL FUNDS

Mutual funds are currently one of the most popular vehicles in which to invest. They also happen to be one of the easiest forms of investing. That is, of course, both the good news and bad news. The good news is it that is easy for investors to get involved in a whole array of investment vehicles. The bad news is that because it is so easy to invest in mutual funds, often times you end up disappointed with the outcome, especially if you don't understand how this type of investment really works.

Mutual funds are neither risky nor safe. It is the type of mutual fund that decides the risk level.

When someone invests in a mutual fund, that investor, along with all the other investors of that fund, pool their money in order to buy more of several different investments. This provides for greater diversification and allows the small investor the opportunity to either invest in companies they could not afford, or are unfamiliar how to purchase. For every mutual fund there is a manager that is in charge of what the fund buys and sells. The good managers are very well known and can be easily researched, along with the funds they manage.

A *Mutual Fund Family* is a group of mutual funds with several different objectives all under one company. For example, the *Franklin Fund Group* is a large mutual fund family. Under the Franklin family there are over thirty different types of mutual funds from which to choose, depending on your investment needs.

The popularity of mutual funds is the result of many fine points of investing. First, it is easy to invest in them and it requires little effort. Then, once you are in the fund, you receive regular statements. You can reinvest your dividends or receive them on a routine, monthly basis. Investors who have been in mutual funds for long periods of time and reinvest all of their dividends are often pleasantly surprised to see exactly how much the fund has grown in value.

Although there are many different funds, they all basically work like this: You or your advisor sends the application along with a check to the fund family. This application is found in the prospectus which should be read and understood before investing. Sometimes having an advisor fill out the forms for you makes sense because he or she is in a better position to know the best time to invest. It may also make the paperwork easier on you.

Once your money is received by the fund, the share price is that day's closing price. So, if you invest in a growth fund and the market happened to be up the day you invested, your fund was probably up too. Let's assume the price is $15 per share and you want to invest $20,000 – you will have purchased 1,333.33 shares. Now let's assume the growth fund that you bought performs well and the share price rises to $20 per share. Although you still have the same number of shares, you can now sell your shares back to the fund for $20 each. In that scenario you made a profit of $6,666.60.

If you were to invest in more of an income-type fund, bond fund, or U.S. government fund, usually the rise in share price is secondary to the dividends you will receive. Many people invest simply to receive the dividends on a monthly basis. That is their income, and hopefully the share price will rise with the cost of living to maintain purchasing power. However, you do not have to take the dividends as income. You can always reinvest them and buy more shares.

WHAT TYPE OF MUTUAL FUNDS ARE MOST POPULAR WITH RETIREES?

Depending on your objectives and the amount of homework you do, you can probably find the type of mutual fund that meets your objectives. Mutual funds range from funds that will only invest in companies that are environmentally friendly, to funds that will only invest in U.S. government bonds, Ginnie Maes, utilities, corporate bonds, or companies that are only part of the Dow Jones Industrial Average. There are companies that invest only in bonds of foreign countries or in junk bonds overseas. In essence, there is a different fund for almost any objective.

Even though there are literally hundreds of fund groups to choose from, mature Americans can probably find what they need in a fund within a core group of possibly five funds in one family.

Remember, all investments have risk. Be sure to read the prospectus and consult a professional.

MONEY MARKETS

Money Market Funds are usually the funds that most resemble a passbook savings account. The share price usually does not fluctuate. Typically, you buy it for a dollar per share and sell it for a dollar per share. Most money markets invest in short-term instruments comprised of very safe securities such as Treasury bills, overnight federal funds and investments similar to those a bank might use for investing CD deposits. These funds usually offer free checking accounts and pay a competitive interest rate. Some money markets are insured, others are not.

The main difference between a money market and a savings account is that a savings account at a bank will usually use your money to invest in securities as short as two to ten days. In contrast, a money market mutual fund might purchase securities with 30-day maturities. For the longer maturity, the yield is better and all the securities purchased in a money market are either government-issued or insured. This is the safest type of fund. Most people use these as a liquid savings account.

UNITED STATES GOVERNMENT BOND FUNDS

As the name implies, these funds usually will only invest in bonds that are either issued by the United States government, backed by the government or one of its various agencies. The main reason to invest in this type of bond is the safety factor. The second reason to invest in a government fund is the usually higher dividend. If a CD is paying 6%, these funds could be paying 8%.

The important point to remember is that these securities do, in fact, pay dividends. If you plan to keep this fund forever and only use the dividends, the share price is a secondary concern. However, ***the share price does fluctuate.*** Just because it is a government fund does not mean you cannot lose money. The biggest factor affecting the share price of a government fund is a change in the interest rate.

For example, assume you invest in a government bond fund paying a dividend of 8%. This sounds pretty good. Assume you invest $50,000 at a share price of $10 – you have purchased 5,000 shares. Now, assume that over the course of the year you received the 8% dividend for income, which is $4,000 for the year, or $333 per month. This is not bad, however, because during the year interest rates rose and your share price dropped. Now, at the end of the year you wish to sell the fund. The share price is now $9.50 per share. Will you get your money back? At $9.50 per share, the 5,000 shares you have are worth only $47,500 of the $50,000 you invested. So, let's add the $4,000 of income the fund generated – that is a total of $51,500. Over the year you made $1,500. My point is that although your dividend was 8%, your total return for the year was actually 3%.

This illustrates why the share price is secondary if you plan to hold the fund forever. Don't forget that everything is cyclical. If you keep the fund for a long period of time, interest rates will cyclically rise and fall and your share price will move with these market cycles. There will be times when you could sell the fund for more then you paid and times when you would sell for less. Although past history is no sure indication of future investment performance, it does show that, over time, the share price will probably slowly rise with the economic environment. The issue that should be your main interest is that, without having to worry, you receive a competitive interest check in your mailbox every month.

The most difficult part of investing is self-discipline. Most investors do not reap the benefits of worry-free interest checks because they are preoccupied with the price per share of their fund during market cycles. Remember your objectives. Remember your plan and stick to it. Also, remember to dollar-cost-average whenever possible.

There are many types of government funds. As discussed earlier, when interest rates rise, the share price of most bond funds will drop. Although most funds are liquid and you can sell them whenever you want, the maturity dates of the bonds that your fund buys will vary. To earn the highest interest rate, some government funds buy long-term (as high as thirty years) government bonds. These long-term bonds pay the highest interest. Conversely, because the bonds are long-term, their share prices are most affected by interest rates.

To stabilize the share price in a rising interest rate environment, you can purchase funds that only invest in short, or intermediate maturity government bonds. Although the interest rate will probably not be as high a long-term bond, the share price is much more stable.

No one can predict when interest rates will rise or fall. Diversification whenever possible is always advisable. For those dollars that may not be needed for a while, a long-term fund would protect current interest rates. For those assets that may be needed more quickly, look for a fund that invests in shorter maturity bonds. The interest may not be as high, but the price per share is usually less volatile.

Remember: Make sure to read the prospectus and ask the average maturity length of the portfolio.

TAX-FREE MUTUAL FUNDS

Although the merits of tax-free investing are studied in the tax chapter, these funds do serve their purpose among retirees. Just like any other types of funds there are AAA-rated, excellent tax-free funds and there are junk tax-free funds. Do your homework. Know the average maturity of the bonds inside the fund and make sure a tax-free investment is right for you.

As discussed under the bonds section, most bonds issued by municipalities, states, and other agencies are tax free. This means the interest that is generated is free of all federal tax. In addition, if you purchase the bonds of the state where you are a resident, the bonds are free of both federal and state taxes. Obviously, this could be a benefit if you are in a high tax bracket and would like tax-free interest.

THERE ARE SOME PRECAUTIONS:

1. Since the bond is tax-free, the interest is lower then what a normal taxable bond would return (like a government bond). Now you must figure out which fund would be better after all taxes and fees: a lower-yield bond with no tax, or a high-yield bond after you pay the taxes. (See taxable equivalent yield formula in the chapter on Taxes.)

2. Although the bonds are tax-free, some are AAA-rated and insured while others are non-rated or lower rated. These bonds can default just like the bond of a private corporation. Many tax-free bond funds buy revenue bonds. For example, suppose a bond is financing a toll bridge. If no one uses the bridge, the bonds could default and you, the bondholder, will not receive the interest. You must be certain the bond fund in which you decide to invest has the right risk category for you. Be wary of too high of a yield, it could be from one of the funds that does not invest in AAA-rated bonds.

3. Just as with government funds, you have interest rate risk. If interest rates rise, your share price could drop in value. Know the maturity date of the bond to track its value.

4. Of special note to seniors is the fact that although the interest rate is tax free, the income generated from the fund is still calculated into your gross income for Social Security purposes. The result is that the income generated could bring you over the limit and your Social Security benefits might be taxed. In addition, tax-free bonds and bond funds are a preference item for the ALTERNATIVE MINIMUM TAX (AMT). The AMT is an additional tax you have to pay if your income ration falls into a certain category and you did not pay enough taxes on the income in relation to the type of income you received.

INCOME FUNDS

This type of fund invests primarily to generate income by way of dividends and keeps the share price more stable than a growth fund. To accomplish this the fund might purchase income-producing stocks such as preferred or convertible stocks, or it might purchase stocks with high dividends such as utilities. But for the most part these funds purchase government agency and corporate bonds.

All in all the funds serve a purpose. What many people do is take only the income they need (such as the amount a CD would give them) and reinvest the rest. The fund usually will not experience growth like a growth fund, but they should experience some growth. And, since the dividends are usually higher, by reinvesting a portion, the shares in your fund build up quicker. This could be considered a good inflation-fighting technique. However, much like a bond or bond fund, if interest rates rise, your share price could drop.

GROWTH FUNDS

A growth fund rarely has a dividend or any source of income. Rather, the objective is to increase the share price by picking investments that will rise in value. Most investments are in stocks of various types. You can find anything from aggressive growth funds to long-term growth funds.

Although many mature Americans ask why they should be investing in growth, the answer is simple: We are living longer then ever before experienced, or expected, after retirement. To compensate, we need to have some growth, to not only maintain the value of our principal but to, in fact, increase it. Again, we have not seen high inflation for a while but everything is cyclical. It will be back and it will rear its ugly head. Even an inflation level as low as 4% to 5% could devastate a retirement over many years if not planned for properly.

The most common reason why people lose money in growth funds is the lack of discipline. Everything is cyclical. There will be up times and down times. Reconsider before selling your fund after the market drops and the share price goes down. Consider averaging in more money at that point. If you are not a long-term investor or disciplined investor, a growth fund might not work for you.

The interesting fact is that most growth funds over any ten year period have outperformed cash returns on savings or money market accounts. Then, why do so many people lose money on growth funds? Again, the answer lies in lack of education and understanding.

Investors sell after a market crashes when they probably should be buying more because they get frustrated in a bad economic period and sell. Sometimes they are convinced by a broker to put their money elsewhere, or they forget that the fund was bought with a long-term prospective. Perhaps someone is touting a new investment at a time when your discipline level is at a low ebb and you can be persuaded to switch your investment.

There should only be a handful of reasons, and never excuses, to sell a fund and none of the above are among them.

GROWTH AND INCOME FUNDS

These funds are an interesting combination of both growth funds and income funds. In essence, they are a hybrid. As mature Americans realize they are living longer and will need more money then originally expected, these will undoubtedly become more popular.

A *Growth and Income Fund* consists of traditional investments found in a growth fund such as stocks, but the objective is to provide consistent monthly income as well. The income is derived from the dividends and bonds that are purchased inside the fund. Hopefully, the stocks will also appreciate in value, thereby increasing the share price.

The need for these funds is huge. People need growth and they need income. If the income is the same as a CD rate or better and the growth from the share price is at all on the plus side, then you are doing better by accomplishing both points – increasing your capital to keep up with inflation and receiving the income you need.

SECTOR FUNDS

Sector Funds are, in my opinion, volatile funds which should usually be avoided. A sector fund will invest in a specific asset class with a specific purpose. You could find sector funds that will only invest in Mexican stocks or others that will only invest in automobile stocks.

The scary thing about sector funds is that they can be the biggest winners one year and the biggest losers the next. You are risking so much in one little sliver of the market that it almost defeats the purpose of the mutual fund – diversification. Wall Street might favor one class of stocks during the year and run their prices up higher than their value should be. Then the market will realize the prices are too high and a large correction may erase much of the profit.

A *Utility Mutual Fund* is one sector fund that I would consider, but only as part of a long-term strategy. Utility funds invest in stocks and bonds of public utility companies. Utility companies do not usually go out of business, so the degree of safety is higher. Be sure the utility fund is one that invests in high quality utilities, and avoid those that invest heavily in utility companies using nuclear power, or other experimental sources of energy.

Utilities usually grow with inflation and usually don't beat the market, but they also don't suffer as much when the market is down. In addition, utilities are a good source of income. Some utilities pay over 7% to 8% dividends. The downside of utilities are the fact that they are very interest sensitive. If interest rates rise, the share price of the fund could drop as a result of declining utility stock prices.

Certain other sector funds could make sense as a part of a diversification technique for an entire portfolio, if for some reason you like a specific sector and want to invest in it. Do thorough research and limit your exposure to no more than the 10% of your portfolio you have already decided you could afford to lose, if it came to that.

CLOSED END VS. OPEN END FUNDS

OPEN END FUNDS

Most investors seem to purchase *Open End Funds.* These funds continually raise more money and rarely close to new investors. Conceivably, such funds could continue unlimited growth in the number of investors and size. When you buy a share of an open end mutual fund, it is done through the mutual fund company and they issue you the shares. When selling the shares, you sell them back to the company, never are they sold on the market like a stock.

THERE ARE SEVERAL REASONS WHY OPEN END FUNDS ARE POPULAR:

1. It is easier to continually advertise open end funds and make investors aware of them.

2. You do not have to go through a broker to buy and sell shares; it can be done directly through the mutual fund company.

3. When dealing directly with the fund it is easier to obtain information and you have greater flexibility as to how and when you take income and other services that might be offered.

CLOSED END FUNDS

Think of a closed end fund much like a stock. Usually when they are in the money-raising stage you will see lots of advertisements and publicity like the *Initial Public Offering (IPO)* of a stock. Unlike an open end fund it does not continually offer shares. Once the offering price is raised, the fund is closed to new investors.

Next, the fund becomes like a stock and trades on an exchange. And, like a stock, buying and selling is very easy. At this point you usually have to go through a broker, unless that particular fund family has a system set up to buy or sell directly. The share price now becomes directly linked to supply and demand. If the stocks in that fund go up, more investors will probably want some of that fund, driving the share price up.

THERE ARE SEVERAL REASONS WHY SOME INVESTORS PREFER CLOSED END FUNDS:

1. If the fund cannot issue more shares, the demand for existing ones will rise faster, especially if the manager performs well. At least that is the theory.

2. Some people feel that if an open end mutual fund does well and many people continually want to invest, the manager of that fund will not be able to efficiently manage the portfolio no matter how good he or she may be. Imagine being a manager of a municipal bond fund that does well. Millions of dollars comes in every day for you to invest. The prospectus might say that you can only have 10% of the total funds assets in cash at any given time. So, by prospectus, you must invest those funds. But what if there are no excellent bond purchases at that time? It does not matter, you have to buy bonds. So the thought is, funds that continually issue new shares get too big for their own good.

3. When investing in a brand new closed end fund (while in the stage of raising the money), the share price will be decided in advance. Figured in to that offering price are usually the underwriting fees and the brokerage fee that entices brokers to sell it. Some people believe that if you wait until all the money is raised and the fund begins to trade on the market, the investor can purchase it for less because the share price will get discounted by the amount of the fees. Although this does not always happen, it is worth considering.

HOW TO READ THE MUTUAL FUND PROSPECTUS

If you have ever studied investing in a mutual fund, you have heard the faithful words, read the *Mutual Fund Prospectus.* But if you have ever tried, you quickly discovered you could read it three times and not learn anything because of the legal jargon. However, there is good information to be learned from it.

Before actually reading the prospectus, view the date on the document. If it is not the most recent one, you might not be receiving all of the critical, updated information. If the fund allows privileges, be sure you are allowed to write checks in the denominations that are comfortable for you. Some might only allow ten checks a month to be written, or have a $1,000 minimum. Also find out the minimum required to invest. If the minimum is $5,000 and you wanted to invest $1,000, go no further.

WHAT TO LOOK FOR IN THE PROSPECTUS:

1.   REQUIRED STATEMENTS

Make certain the prospectus has language something like this and any representation to the contrary is a criminal offense: *These securities have not been approved or disapproved by the Securities and Exchange Commission (SEC) nor has the Commission passed upon the accuracy or adequacy or this prospectus.*

If the prospectus says something to the effect that the security has been approved by the SEC, then it is a false document. The SEC does not approve or disapprove any security, it merely registers them. The prospectus should also state that you may obtain a copy of the *Statement of Additional Information.* This is almost like a continuation of the prospectus going into more detail. All investors are entitled to a copy upon request.

2.   FUND OBJECTIVE

You should see some kind of statement outlining the objective of the fund. For example, a mutual fund might be named the ABC Dynamic Great Fund. Your friends have told you how wonderful it is, so you called to order the prospectus. Under the fund objective, there might be a statement describing it as an aggressive growth fund seeking high capital appreciation through the investments in companies under $10,000,000 in size. If you were not aware you were investing in an aggressive growth fund, the objective section of the prospectus makes that clear.

3. FUND FEE

Within the first few pages of the prospectus you should find a fee table in which the fees are broken down. First it should tell you the front-sales charge, if any. The sales load is usually a one-time, up-front charge that is paid by the investor for buying the fund. The charge is expressed as a percentage of the amount invested. It would also tell you if there is a charge or fee to sell the funds as well.

Breaking the expenses down further will show the annual expenses such as management fees and 12b-1 fees. The total will tell you how much per year the fund is charging you. Finally, you should note any one-time fees such as switching funds into the family or charges to wire money to your bank.

4. FUND PERFORMANCE

Somewhat buried in the heart of the prospectus will be fund performance information, either explained or detailed in a graph. It might give you recent yield figures, performance on a year-to-year basis and cumulative return since inception of the fund.

5. FUND PROVISIONS AND POLICIES

It is in this section that you will learn what the fund is and is not allowed to do. For example, if you purchase a government bond fund thinking the fund only invests in government bonds, this section of the prospectus will tell you exactly how much of the fund's total dollars actually have to be invested in government bonds. You will learn if they can invest in other types of bonds and if they are required to have certain maturities. Do you want a fund that can only buy maturities of bonds in excess of twenty years? Or, what if the government bond fund you purchased needs only to have 30% of the portfolio in government bonds?

6. FUND RISK

This is the section that will tell you the level of risk you are taking – if you can lose money and how you can lose money. It will break down the risk into several areas.

First, it might tell you the risk of the type of securities in the fund. The second type of risk might be regarding how the manager directs the fund. In other words, the provisions of the prospectus might allow the manager of a particular fund to *Write Naked Options.* This might increase the risk of a fund. A third risk that could be detailed in the prospectus is economic risk and market cycle information.

7. FUND FAMILY

Somewhere in the prospectus you will find information about the mutual fund family that is offering that particular fund. The fund family is usually also know as the *Investment Advisor.* In this section you should learn about how long the family has been in business, who they use for accounting, where the home office is located and possibly telephone numbers to use. This information should give you a better perception as to how established the company may be.

8. SHAREHOLDER RIGHTS

Despite popular belief, the shareholder has rights as an investor. Almost without exception the first is the right to vote. Usually you will be allowed one vote for every share you own. You may vote on such issues as management compensation, investment policies and the issuance of more shares. A complete breakdown of your voting rights can be found in this section. Also, your rights if you have a complaint should also be found in this section. The most common right is that you have the right to arbitration if a dispute arises.

9. FUND EARNINGS

Many mutual funds such as a money market or Treasury funds will pay the shareholder dividends. It should be important for you to know how these dividends are declared and paid. Many people find it a criteria that the fund declares these dividends daily and pays them monthly. It will be your choice if you want the dividend check sent to you every month, or reinvested into the fund to purchase more shares. Note that typical growth funds will not declare dividends daily, or pay them monthly.

10.   TAXES OF FUNDS

If a mutual fund declares any kind of distribution such as a dividend or capital gain, you, the shareholder, must report this on your income tax return. Usually you will know the amount through a 1099 tax statement that the mutual fund is required to send to you. Even tax-free returns should be noted on your tax return. There is a place on your tax return for this information.

11.   HOW TO BUY AND REDEEM SHARES

This section will tell you if you should call the company directly or go through a broker. It will also tell you the requirement of selling the fund. Sometimes you will be required to write a letter; other times they will liquidate by phone. Regardless, you should be aware before investing so there are no surprises later.

Obviously the prospectus goes into much greater detail and you should read the entire document thoroughly. If you still require more information, call the company or your financial advisor. Also, you can request a Statement of Additional Information.

HOW TO CHOOSE A MUTUAL FUND

Unfortunately, most people do not receive the kinds of returns that many mutual funds quote. The reason is obvious – the average person is not clear on how to correctly buy or sell a mutual fund. Because it is so popular and easy to invest in funds and so many newsletters and magazines give you their opinion on which are the best funds, it often affects your decision. Remember, newspapers and newsletters can give you statistics on a particular fund, but they do not know what is right for you. Only you, your financial plan and your advisors can determine that.

One of the most important ingredients in picking a fund is to determine your objective. What are you trying to accomplish? Don't worry about what your neighbor, cousin, or friend is doing. Go back to square one and try to decide what is it that you are trying to accomplish. Before investing, review the sections on financial planning and asset allocation.

Picking a mutual fund is not an easy task. Sometimes I wish it were as difficult to invest in a fund as it is to learn how to properly invest in one. Since it is so easy to invest in, many people do not do the research necessary and end up disappointed.

If you follow these basic ten points for picking a mutual fund and learn how to interpret the information you receive, the odds of your being pleased with your investment decision, or at least understanding what you are doing, is greatly enhanced.

THE 10-POINT CHECK LIST FOR SELECTING A MUTUAL FUND:

1.   YOUR OBJECTIVE

If all you need is an 8% return, don't concern yourself with searching top performers because they are usually the most risky. Forget what your friend says or what an advertisement reads – you should always know your objective first.

2.   PERFORMANCE

Not only do you ask what the 1, 3, 5 and 10 year annualized returns are, but know the performance during every year. Be watching for how the fund performed during years that the market did poorly. Good funds perform better then the market in down years.

3.   RISK

This is one of the most critical areas to research. Your fund might have returned 20%, but how much risk did you take? If you could have made 15% with one-third of the risk, which fund would you have used?

Risk and volatility is measured by using *Beta, Alpha* and *Standard Deviation.* The Standard and Poor's 500 is the benchmark and is automatically assigned a beta of "1." If your fund has a beta greater then one, your fund will be more volatile and possibly more risky then the S&P 500.

For example, if the S&P 500 is down 10% and your mutual fund has a bet of 1.5%, your mutual fund could very well be down 15% when the market is down 10%. However, if your mutual fund has a beta of only 5%, if the market is down 10%, your fund might only be down 5%. So ideally, you would want to find a mutual fund with as low of a beta as possible, but one which has returns as close to that of the market or better, if you are trying to achieve growth. Obviously, a government bond fund, or something like that, would not receive the return of the market, but you would want a very low beta.

The *Alpha* is the measure of how your fund did compared to the market. If over a period of one year the market was flat (if you invested $10,000 and 12 months later your money was worth $10,000) what would your fund have produced? If your fund would have been flat, like the market, your fund would have a "0" alpha. The higher the alpha the better your fund would have done against the market.

So, unlike the beta, you want a high alpha. A negative alpha would indicate your fund would have lost money if the market was flat. The higher the alpha, the better your fund would have done. Ideally, if you were comparing mutual funds you would want the highest alpha, with the lowest beta and the best return.

4.   TOP FUND HOLDINGS

Do you know which companies your fund owns and do you agree with their choices? If the fund invests too much in a few select companies, or if you don't like the companies, then consider if you would want that fund.

5.   PROSPECTUS PROVISIONS

When reading the prospectus (something you should always do) you should find out what the manager is allowed to do with your money. Figure out if it has to be fully in stocks or bonds at all times, or can it simply hold cash. Can it buy options and future contracts? If so, does this lower or raise the risk of the fund?

6.   FUND MANAGER

How long has the fund manager managed? If a fund boasts large returns, it does not mean all that much if the manager is brand new. What is the track record of the manager? How long has he or she been at the company and where did he or she manage previously?

7.   FUND FAMILY

Invest in a family of funds with many strong performers. People's goals change and if you stay in one family, usually fees are reduced and paperwork is simplified.

8.   SIZE OF FUND

Bigger funds are not necessarily better. Many funds get too large and cannot find a way to prudently invest all the money. I find that problem with many tax-free bond funds. They get so big, with so much money, they cannot properly invest all the money coming into them.

9.   FUND EXPENSES

I like to know how much the fund is charging me. Don't misunderstand me, if I have a fund with expenses that are higher then average, it is not bad if they are making me more money then other funds. If not, then I go into a fund with fewer expenses. Look at all the other criteria first, then look at the expenses. The bottom line is, where will I make more money net of all fees and charges? If you are a long term investor and a loaded fund (one that has a front-charge), is superior to a no-load, don't worry so much about not paying the load. Over a period of years, the fee becomes insignificant. Look first at which is the better fund.

10.   MARKET/INTEREST SENSITIVE

This indicates what will happen to the fund if the market drops or interest-sensitive funds (government, tax-free or utilities), have interest rates go the wrong way. In the first few years of the 1990s, interest rates dropped dramatically. Thus, the total return of many interest-sensitive funds was very good. If interest rates begin to rise, those funds will probably not be able to show the same kind of returns. Yet, they might use advertising showing the last few years' returns being very high. However, you know that although they did well, in periods of rising interest rates, the funds' prospective now changes.

Obviously, picking a mutual fund is not the easiest thing. And just because you properly select a fund doesn't ensure that you will make money. Half the battle is picking the right fund, the other half is your investment disposition.

The important point is that once you pick the fund, give it time to perform. If the market drops and your fund goes down, consider averaging in more money. Maintain discipline. Seriously review your decision before selling and taking a loss. Unless something fundamental changes in your plan, or in the particular fund in which you have invested, give it room and time to do what you want it to do. It is good to track your fund and I would encourage graphing as well. But if you watch it on a daily basis, it will probably drive you crazy.

MUTUAL FUND COMPARISON

In referring to the two mutual funds graphs shown, much needs to be discussed.

You will note that the ABC fund is the more popular mutual fund, praised in all the newspapers (hypothetically speaking). The obvious reason is because of its spectacular performance. Over ten years, 17.15% annualized, over five years, 26%, and over three years, 27%. However, what risk did you take for that return? Notice under "Fund Objective" this is an aggressive growth fund. Also, notice under "Annual Total Returns," it has returned as low as a -18.93%.

In further reviewing the risk level of the fund, we refer to the beta and the alpha. The current beta of this fund is 1.59. This means if the Standard and Poor's has a beta of 1, this is more volatile and has a greater propensity for risk than a fund with a beta less than the benchmark (The Standard and Poor's 500).

Also defined is the alpha. The higher the alpha; the higher the beta. This particular fund's alpha is higher than the average of most aggressive growth funds.

However, the standard deviation is quite high, which means you will take on much risk for the return that is generated.

Finally, review the expenses of the fund and the returns after the fee and loads to see if an investor can still make money after the fund.

In comparing XYZ fund, consider the same criteria.

The performance figures are almost identical. Over the short-term, ABC fund has outperformed XYZ fund. As a result, most investors may be inclined to purchase ABC first. However, notice XYZ is considered a long-term growth fund, not an aggressive fund. The lowest one-year performance (1984) was 8.27%.

You will notice that the beta is almost identical to the benchmark S&P 500, thereby reducing your risk and volatility. That is one reason the standard deviation is so much lower than the ABC fund, meaning the risk/reward ratio is more in line. (After all, you want a low standard deviation.) In addition, the alpha is higher than fund ABC, which means fund XYZ is performing better in a flat market.

Finally, consider the returns after all expenses and loads. Fund XYZ might not be considered because of its low 3% load, but don't discount it. The ongoing expense ratios are lower, and the returns after all charges are not that much different.

MUTUAL FUND ABC

OBJECTIVE............................AGGRESSIVE GROWTH
ADDRESS..............................4500 MAIN ST., KANSAS CITY, MO 64111
TELEPHONE..........................(816) 555-5575, (800) 555-2021
FUND MANAGER..................,..NAME OF FUND MANAGER
NAV 02/26-93......................$16.68
FUND SYMBOL.......................ABC
TOTAL NET ASSETS...............$5,299,285,000
YEAR ORGANIZED..................1957

FUND PERFORMANCE SUMMARY
AS OF 02/26/93
(Based on NAV With Distribution Reinvested)

	Total Percent Return	Annualized Percent Return	Performance Ranking in the Aggressive Growth Category (1=Top 10% 10=Bottom 10%)
3 Months Total Return	0.18		7th Decile
1 Year Total Return	-3.86	-3.86	9th Decile
3 Year Total Return	112.59	28.58	1st Decile
5 Year Total Return	183.86	23.20	1st Decile
10 Year Total Return	296.85	14.78	2nd Decile

ANNUAL TOTAL RETURNS:

1983	26.28%	1988	13.32%
1984	-18.93%	1989	36.94%
1985	26.17%	1990	9.36%
1986	10.26%	1991	86.45%
1987	6.69%	1992	1.27%

MUTUAL FUND ABC
HYPOTHETICAL $10,000 INVESTMENT AFTER MAXIMUM
FRONT-END LOAD AND DISTRIBUTIONS REINVESTED
(AS OF 2/26/93)

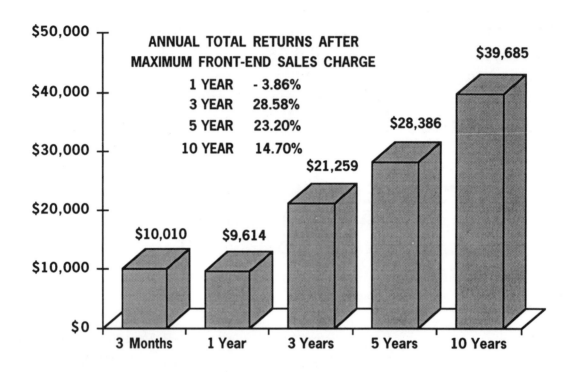

Annual Total Returns After Maximum Front-End Sales Charge

1 Year..-3.86%
3 Year...28.58%
5 Year...23.20%
10 Year... 14.78%

Minimum Investment ....Initial 0		Subsequent Investment....................$0	
Maximum Front-End Load .... 0.00% (NL)		Maximum Back-End Load................(None)	
12 B-1 Fees (12/31/91) ....(Not Apr'd)		Expense Ratio (10/31/91) 1.00%	
Turnover Ratio (12/91) 42.00		Average Maturity ....N/A	
Alpha 0.57		Beta..1.57	
Standard Deviation 7.62		No. of Monthly Observations.............36	

Information contained herein is based on sources and data believed reliable, but is not guaranteed by the author and is not to be construed as a solicitation of an offer to buy or sell securities mentioned herein. Data quoted represents past performance. Investment values will fluctuate so that an investor's shares, when redeemed, may be worth more or less than their original cost.

MUTUAL FUND XYZ

OBJECTIVE........................LONG-TERM GROWTH

ADDRESS..........................82 DEVONSHIRE ST., BOSTON, MA 02109

TELEPHONE......................(801) 555-1910, (800) 555-8888

FUND MANAGER................NAME OF FUND MANAGER

NAV 02/26-93..................$28.25

FUND SYMBOL...................XYZ

TOTAL NET ASSETS...........$1,974,200,000

YEAR ORGANIZED.............1963

FUND PERFORMANCE SUMMARY
AS OF 02/26/93
(Based on NAV With Distribution Reinvested)

	Total Percent Return	Annualized Percent Return	Performance Ranking in the Aggressive Growth Category (1=Top 10% 10=Bottom 10%)
3 Months Total Return..........	6.55		.... 2nd Decile
1 Year Total Return	13.34	13.34	.... 2nd Decile
3 Year Total Return	100.48	26.09	.... 1st Decile
5 Year Total Return	201.68	24.71	.... 1st Decile
10 Year Total Return	389.56	17.21	.... 1st Decile

ANNUAL TOTAL RETURNS:

1983	.........................23.28%	1988	........................21.02%
1984	...........................-8.27%	1989	........................43.15%
1985	.........................27.06%	1990	.........................3.94%
1986	.........................13.32%	1991	........................54.92%
1987	...........................-1.90%	1992	........................15.89%

MUTUAL FUND XYZ
HYPOTHETICAL $10,000 INVESTMENT AFTER MAXIMUM
FRONT-END LOAD AND DISTRIBUTIONS REINVESTED
(AS OF 2/26/93)

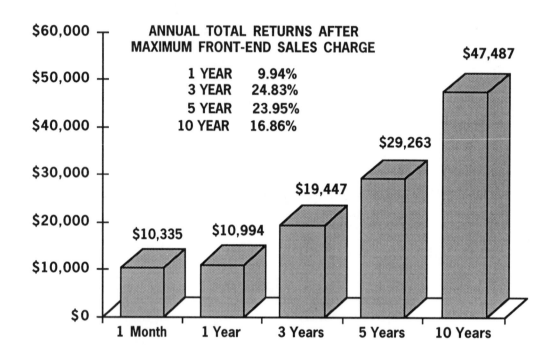

Annual Total Returns After Maximum Front-End Sales Charge

1 Year..9.94%
3 Year..24.82%
5 Year..23.95%
10 Year...16.86%

Minimum Investment ....Initial $2,500
Maximum Front-End Load .... 3.00% (LL)
12 B-1 Fees (12/31/91) ....(Not Apr'd)
Turnover Ratio (12/91) 217.00
Alpha 0.86
Standard Deviation 4.41

Subsequent Investment $250
Maximum Back-End Load ....(None)
Expense Ratio (12/31/91) 0.89%
Average Maturity ....N/A
Beta 1.02
No. of Monthly Observations 36

Information contained herein is based on sources and data believed reliable, but is not guaranteed by the author and is not to be construed as a solicitation of an offer to buy or sell securities mentioned herein. Data quoted represents past performance. Investment values will fluctuate so that an investor's shares, when redeemed, may be worth more or less than their original cost.

UNIT INVESTMENT TRUSTS

Over the last several years, *Unit Investment Trusts (UITs)* have been gaining in popularity and probably for good reason.

Think of a UIT as a bond. It has a specific offering price and a set maturity date and price. UITs are very much like mutual funds in that your money is pooled with that of several other investors to make a larger investment at a better price. They are also similar to mutual funds in that the trusts may own several different investments for diversification. Instead of buying one bond, you are buying one trust with several bonds, or stocks, in it.

The various types of UITs are almost as numerous as types of mutual funds. A few in particular seem to make good sense in these economic times. Because a UIT has a set maturity date, you are usually insured to receive a fixed interest rate, provided you hold it until maturity. The maturity date can range from one year up to 30 years. Most trusts are liquid so that if you need your money, you can sell at any time. The catch is that you will get whatever price the market is paying. You might make money or you might lose money.

Unlike a mutual fund, the interest from a UIT is set and your monthly check will probably be the same every month, *making this a good vehicle for current income since it is easier to budget.* The reason the interest does not fluctuate is because once the securities in the trust are purchased, they are held. UITs do not continually buy and sell like a mutual fund, nor does money come in every day from new investors. After the securities are purchased, the UIT closes at a specific offering price and is held for the life of a trust, which leads to another advantage of a trust.

Since the securities are not continually bought and sold, once the securities are purchased, there is really no ongoing management. Consequently, there is either no continuing management fee or it is minimal. In the case of an AAA-rated GNMA trust, because it does not have a management fee and because it purchased the GNMAs in large amounts, then the yield to the investor is probably higher than a comparable GNMA fund. This means your monthly check should be higher. Think of it ... if your trust bought ten-year GNMAs and a mutual fund had ten-year GNMAs, which is most likely to enjoy a higher yield? The trust. Of course, the advantage to a mutual fund is that there is an active manager to continually buy and sell the GNMAs trying to make money as the GNMAs are bought and sold. However, every investor's portfolio should have certain securities that are guaranteed where the interest rate is known and it is certain how much money will be earned. If interest rates drop, you can make money if the trust is sold. But at least you are assured your interest will not drop. Conversely, if interest rates rise, you do not have to worry about the price of your trust because you can hold it until maturity and are guaranteed your money back.

Although there are many kinds of trusts, I am really only focusing on the highest quality, safest trusts.

YOUR CRITERIA IN SEARCHING FOR HIGH QUALITY, SAFE TRUSTS:

1.   SAFETY

This is done preferably by rating. Make sure the vehicle is AAA-rated and insured, usually by an individual insurance company that specializes in insuring trusts.

2.   TYPE OF TRUST

I mostly work with high quality GNMA trusts, Treasury security trusts, tax-free municipal trusts, or possibly utility trusts. What I like about a utility trust is that you can see in advance which utility stocks or bonds the trust owns, analyze the interest rate and decide if it is what you want. In addition, as many of you know, most utilities pay interest quarterly. If you want monthly interest you must buy four different utility stocks, each paying a dividend at a different time. In the case of a trust, they have already performed this task, and you enjoy monthly interest.

3.   MATURITY

Although the interest may be good, you should plan to hold it until it matures. As a result, all of your investments should not be in long-term maturities. They should be staggered, depending on your plan, goals and the interest rates offered.

4.   FEES

Many of these trusts have no management fee, but you should be certain of this before buying. Also, know if there are liquidation (redemption) fees and a load. Ask what the price is when you buy it, at what price it will mature and what is the current yield. The current yield could be different from the stated coupon yield if you pay more than the offering price or less. If you pay more per share, your current yield would be lower than the stated coupon because you paid more, thereby increasing your yield.

You will hear more about trusts as people continually search for new ways to earn safe money. There will always be those who are afraid of investments that have substantial risk. But the same investors often cannot afford the low rates that banks or CDs pay. The alternative is often the trust.

ANNUITIES

For the mature American, a properly structured annuity could be an excellent investment that provides superior yields and guarantees, a terrific estate planning tool, a way to curve taxes and something that is not to difficult to understand. If my hunch is correct, annuities will soon be almost as common a tool as mutual funds are currently. Of course, the trick is your understanding of them to make sure they are properly structured on your behalf.

WHAT IS AN ANNUITY?

An *Annuity* is a definition of a financial strategy. Just like a mutual fund, an annuity is neither bad nor good but a type of investment. And depending of the type of annuity it is, it will present the option of investing in many different vehicles, including mutual funds and guaranteed deposit funds similar to a certificate of deposit.

Usually the custodian of your money, or the *Annuity Issuer,* is an insurance company. Don't be confused – although the investment might be in a mutual fund, the issuer of the annuity is still the insurance company.

While the funds stay inside the annuity, your money will grow tax deferred, but if you decide to take income from the interest or earnings, it becomes taxable. If you withdraw the money it is taxable. Think of an annuity like an IRA. First, find an annuity that offers the type of investment you are seeking. You put the money in and it grows tax-deferred. Like an IRA, you cannot take the money without a penalty until your are 59 1/2 years of age. However, unlike an IRA, you do not have to pull out any money at age 70 1/2. You can continue the compounding as long as you wish.

Usually an annuity is broken down into two phases: an *Accumulation Phase* and a *Annuitization Phase.*

ACCUMULATION PHASE

The accumulation phase is the period of time when you put funds in and let them grow. While the funds are in the accumulation phase, they will grow tax deferred. If you start pulling interest or earnings out, you will be taxed. If you *Annuitize*, you are no longer in the accumulation phase, you are now in the annuitization phase. *Do not mistake the annuitization phase with simply taking income.*

ANNUITY PHASE

The annuity phase is mandatory with some companies; with some it is a choice. When you decide to annuitize your annuity, you relinquish all of the money you have in the annuity and it's not your money any more. In return you receive a guaranteed income for a specified period of time, determined by whatever annuity option you have selected – income for the rest of your life for both you and a spouse or a guaranteed number of years. The income will usually be higher then whatever the going rate is and usually it will be partially tax free. We discuss this option more under *Choosing the Annuity Option.*

In addition to these two phases, two major types of annuities exist: *Fixed* and *Variable.*

FIXED ANNUITY

A fixed annuity is insured and pays you a guaranteed rate of return. The guarantee and insurance comes from the insurance company issuing the annuity. This can be good or bad depending on the homework you have done.

THESE STEPS WILL HELP IN YOUR DETERMINATION OF A FIXED ANNUITY:

1. **FIRST, DECIDE IF YOU BELIEVE IN THE INSURANCE COMPANY**

Ask for the rating – AAA by Standard and Poor's is the among the highest. In addition, ask where your funds will be deposited. When you invest in a bank CD and ask where your money will go, I'm not sure if you will get a good answer. But when investing in an annuity, they will tell you where the funds are invested.

Some insurance companies will only place your money in United States government-backed instruments; others will place your funds wherever they choose. Incidentally, this is one reason why the interest rates vary so greatly. If you are confident about the size and quality of the insurance backing your deposit, then maybe you aren't as worried about where your funds are going. If you aren't so sure – find out.

I have never been in a bank or savings and loan and heard customers ask where their CD money will be invested. Yet look at what happened – many banks invested in questionable real estate, made poor investments and are now paying for it. When you invest in an annuity, you will probably get a higher interest rate then the bank - *but it is not FDIC-insured!* So be sure to ask where your money is being invested.

2.   ASK IF YOUR MONEY IS KEPT IN A SEPARATE ACCOUNT.

Because investors are getting smarter, issuers of annuities are making their investments better. If the issuer of the annuity says that funds are kept in a separate account, that means that the deposits from the annuity you invested with are not co-mingled with the general assets of that insurance company, but are kept completely separate. If the insurance company fails, those assets cannot be thrown in with all the other bad assets, or be bait for creditor claims.

3.   FIND OUT HOW INTEREST IS CREDITED AND HOW LONG IT IS GUARANTEED.

You might see an advertisement for an annuity guaranteeing a higher interest rate then you might expect. Often the rate will be guaranteed for one year, but then after one year it will drop to a rate set by the insurance company. But you cannot simply withdraw your money because there will be a penalty for a set number of years (usually between five and ten years).

If you do invest in this type of annuity, ask for a log of interest rates the issuer has paid to investors in the past, after the first year. If they maintain a credible rate, then okay. If not, then reconsider. Incidentally, the "lingo" used by insurance companies is "old money/new money." When you first deposit, your money is new, earning a better rate. Subsequently it is old, earning the lower rate.

Other annuities have no old money/new money acquisition. This means, whatever the new investor receives in interest, the old investor receives. Usually these annuities will readjust their interest rates up or down every quarter depending on the prevailing rates. These annuities probably will not pay you as high of first-year interest, but chances are, over the term of the annuity, you will receive more competitive interest rates. The reason is, they have to pay new investors the same rate that you are earning. To attract new investors, it better be good. Always know in advance what the absolute lowest interest is that your annuity can pay if interest rates plummet. Usually they will have a minimum rate.

4.   ASK WHAT THE PENALTY IS FOR EARLY WITHDRAWAL.

Usually, like a CD-type account, if you withdraw early they will get you. Ask if there are any charges up front. In addition, if you decide to take interest, how often will they pay? Monthly? Quarterly? Semi-annually? Will they charge for this service?

5.   BE CLEAR ON THE ANNUITIZATION.

Do you ever have to annuitize and, if so, when? Is it set by number of years, or your age? If you do have to annuitize, will there be a "bail out option" allowing you to withdraw your money free of penalty before that date? I usually tend to stick with companies that never make an investor annuitize. It might be possible that annuitizing makes sense for you, but it should be a choice, not a requirement.

VARIABLE ANNUITY

A *Variable Annuity* will have most of the characteristics of a fixed annuity with a few major differences. One difference is that the interest rate is not fixed – you choose the investment.

What has been happening lately is that popular mutual fund companies have been teaming up with certain insurance companies to issue variable annuities. The advantage of this is you can invest with your favorite mutual fund company inside a variable annuity.

ADVANTAGES OF A VARIABLE ANNUITY

1. **TAX-DEFERRED GROWTH OF YOUR MUTUAL FUNDS.**

This in itself should either make, or not make all the difference in the world. Assume you invest in a growth and income mutual fund that averages 10% per year in total return (part dividend and part capital gain) and you have been reinvesting for ten years. You originally started with $10,000. You now have $26,000.

However, your investment is taxed every year (you receive a 1099 tax statement). In addition, you will pay taxes on the capital gain on the stock the year you sell. Assume after the tenth year you sell and pay the tax. After all said and done, your after-tax proceeds were about $20,000.

Now assume you invested in the same fund inside the annuity. In ten years you would have the same $26,000, but did not pay taxes every year on the reinvested dividends. Assume you are pleased with the investment, have made enough money and now sell the fund, transferring the proceeds to the money market inside the variable annuity. All the taxable gain is completely deferred.

Even if you sold the annuity and paid the tax, chances are you will have more money. In the first example, outside the annuity, your fund generated dividends and, although your reinvested them, you received a 1099 tax form every year and paid taxes. Depending on the amount of dividends paid, this could take a 10% return down to a true 8.5% return because the taxes you paid reduced your overall gain. The difference of 1.5% compounded over ten years is dramatic.

Inside the annuity, all the dividends are tax deferred until you withdraw, earning you the true 10% return. Imagine if you own a government bond mutual fund, which is mostly dividends and little capital gain. If you make 9% per year in that fund and 8% is dividend, your return after taxes could be (depending on your tax bracket) reduced by over 2% every year. If you do not need the money, consider tax deferral.

Emphasizing the point even further, there is even more to consider for those investors who try to beat the market and use "timed" switches between growth accounts and markets in their mutual funds. If they are doing well, the capital gains must be tremendous. Why not defer them all under the umbrella of an annuity?

2.   **A VARIABLE ANNUITY SIMPLIFIES YOUR INVESTMENTS.**

You might find an annuity that offers many funds of several different popular mutual fund families. Instead of receiving numerous statements from numerous companies, you will receive one consolidated statement.

3.   **MAKE CERTAIN YOUR ASSETS ARE KEPT IN A SEPARATE ACCOUNT.**

As in the case of the fixed annuity, make certain your assets are kept in a separate account, which means the funds are either at the mutual fund company, or in a completely separate account from the issuer of the annuity. If the issuer of the annuity company fails, you don't want your funds to be a part of it.

4.   **MOST VARIABLE ANNUITIES OFFER A GUARANTEE.**

The guarantee states that if you invest in a mutual fund and subsequently pass away, your beneficiaries are guaranteed your original investment at the least. This means if you invested $10,000 and the fund lost money and dropped down to $8,000 before you died, your beneficiary is guaranteed the original $10,000.

COMMON ADVANTAGES AND DISADVANTAGES TO BOTH TYPES OF ANNUITIES

If you are an investor in CDs or mutual funds, and if the money is being rolled over every year, you are still paying taxes. Tax deferral could be a better alternative. *Even if you invest in tax-free accounts, the interest earned is still computed into your gross income for Social Security purposes and will affect the amount of tax paid on Social Security benefits.*

So, if you have a problem with your Social Security being taxed, the income earned in an annuity is not figured into the gross income calculation for Social Security.

We discuss annuities for other reasons, under other sections of the book for estate tax purposes. Technically, the annuity is issued by an insurance company, thereby providing a beneficiary. The beneficiary will receive this asset free of probate.

COMMON DISADVANTAGES

Although the money will be received free of probate to a beneficiary, it will not be free of taxes forever. When the beneficiary sells the annuity, he or she will pay a capital gain on the difference of your original contribution and the value at the time of sale. Annuities will not receive a step up in basis like many other investments that are properly structured to receive one.

Another disadvantage is the fact that you will probably incur a tax penalty if you withdraw prior to age 59 1/2. Make sure this is long-term money. Be sure the company that issues the annuity is solid and will be around longer then you.

ANNUITIZATION

Now the annuity discussion gets tricky. Remember that the annuity has the accumulation phase and the annuitization phase. For those of you that own an annuity, do the following: Get your policy out and read the first page. Note the *Annuity Date or Retirement Date.* Then read the definition in your policy under annuitization.

Assume the annuity is in the accumulation phase. You are probably allowed to add to it, take out funds (perhaps with or without a penalty), possibly even have dividends paid to you, instead of reinvesting. In the annuitization phase, the company who issued the annuity gives you a guaranteed income for a period of time. Your options might be for one lifetime, both your lifetime and your spouse's, or a guaranteed number of years regardless if a person dies.

You must realize that once you annuitize you can never get your money back. It is now the property of the company. If you do close the annuity and withdraw all your money before the annuity date, the contract will probably automatically annuitize.

I stress that people should only annuitize if it makes absolute sense and they have done all the numbers. As much as I like annuities, the annuitizing is hard for me to see work to the investor's benefit in most cases. Several companies are now coming out with annuities that you never have to annuitize. I like these over companies that require you to annuitize.

Annuitizing an annuity might work as follows:

You originally invested $10,000, it is now worth $50,000 and your annuity date is next month. The company sends you a document that reads, "We will be annuitizing your annuity; which option would you prefer? (1) Income for the rest of your life equal to $500 per month, or (2) Income for the remainder of your life and your spouse's life equal to $450 per month?"

Assume you and your spouse are 70 years of age in fairly good health. Which option should you take?

First, the one option not mentioned was to liquidate your money, close the annuity and have them send you a check for $50,000. This option often makes the most sense.

The second option of $500 per month for life sounds wonderful because it is over 12% interest. But think about it. The company issuing the annuity says that based on your mortality, no way will you live past 90. If we pay you $500 per month, which is $6,000 per year for the next twenty years, you will have received a total of $120,000. Sounds like a terrific return. However, when compounded, that is less then a 5% annualized interest rate. It's even less, considering they had access to your money over the 20 years. Remember, you never have access to your principal again.

The same scenario is true for the final option. Obviously these numbers are extreme but they illustrate how one can make a bad decision simply because he or she did not do the numbers.

DO THE NUMBERS – THEY DON'T LIE

In all fairness, situations do exist when the annuity makes sense. Three of these times might be as follows:

1. TAX-FREE INCOME.

When you annuitize, much of the income you receive is tax-free. The company paying you the annuity payments shows on your 1099 tax form as though a large portion of the money is actually your principal being returned. You are not taxed on principal coming back to you. Be sure to figure in the tax benefits when deciding if you should annuitize.

2. AVOID CREDITOR CLAIMS.

Sometimes you can annuitize to avoid creditor claims. If you don't have access to the money, neither do your creditors. They might, however, garnishee the income.

3. MAKE INCOME LAST.

If your estate is extremely large and subject to high estate taxes and you can find no other solution, you may benefit by annuitizing the money and making the income last as long as possible (taking a guaranteed 30-year income option). Your beneficiaries will receive the income as well, even after you have passed away.

CHAPTER 17

Understanding Portfolio Risk and Volatility

As discussed in previous chapters, this is the last component with regards to the investment process. Your financial plan should already be in place and you should have a fairly good understanding of investments. Or, at least understand which ones are right and wrong for you.

When deciding how exactly to diversify your portfolio you must have the answer to a great many questions. It goes without saying – whether you are checking up on your own existing portfolio, have just received your retirement rollover or you are starting from scratch.

GOOD ADVICE FOR INVESTORS:

1. **DON'T CHANGE YOUR PORTFOLIO.**
    Once you allocate and diversify your portfolio in a way that best represents your needs, seriously consider before making any changes to the portfolio for any reason

unless your goals change, or something is seriously wrong with a particular investment you have chosen. Review it, but don't necessarily change the allocation. Usually the more emotional you are about your investments, the lower the returns.

2.   BE WARY OF RECOMMENDATIONS.

Don't invest based only on a friend's recommendation because no one knows your situation or your plan. How can you invest in something someone recommends who does not know your portfolio?

3.   DON'T BORROW MONEY TO INVEST.

4.   NEVER INVEST IN SOMETHING YOU DON'T UNDERSTAND.

If you can't describe the investment in three minutes or less, forget it. Too many investments exist that you probably understand better.

5.   REMEMBER THAT EVERYTHING IS CYCLICAL.

If you are diversified correctly something in your portfolio will probably always be down. If you are not disciplined and sell simply because something is down, you will not be a successful investor.

6.   THINK OF INVESTING AS SMART SHOPPING.

If you can think of investing as buying clothes, your chances of success will be enhanced. If you see something on sale and know it is worth more, buy it. If you like a pair of jeans and buy them, don't return them if they go on sale, buy another pair.

7.   DON'T TRY TO GUESS THE HIGH AND LOW PRICE.

And never put all your money in one thing at one time. Too many people say, "I'll wait until interest rates rise (or go down)," or "I will wait until the market is cheaper before I go in." The problem with this approach is you might never get the price you want and might lose many benefits of long-term investing.

The fact is, if you are a long-term investor, as all investors should be, even if you bought at the worst possible day every year, your return would still be better then a savings account over a ten year period. *Use the dollar-cost-average approach as much as possible.*

The great investors don't risk money they can't afford to lose, they do not put all their eggs in one basket and many times don't often "make a killing" in the market. Instead, a simple, methodical approach usually wins out.

Always revert back to what you are trying to accomplish: *Control, Preservation and Maximization.*

Let's assume we review your financial plan and decide that, to be absolutely safe, your portfolio needs a 9% return. We assume that both of you (a married couple) are going to be retired for another 35 years and you would like to avoid using as much principal as possible. You would like the principal to go to the grandchildren for education.

It does not matter very much how much money the person has in deciding how to allocate; what matters is the 9% return.

IF YOU ALLOCATED CORRECTLY, YOU SHOULD BE ABLE TO ANSWER THESE QUESTIONS:

1. What is my risk level on the entire portfolio?
2. Will I earn my required rate of return?
3. What changes should be made as economic environments change?
4. How can I earn the return I need with the lowest risk?

AVERAGE RETURN AND BETA COEFFICIENT

First, learn how to figure what your portfolio's *Average Expected Return* is and your *Beta Coefficient.*

When reviewing or creating your portfolio, if you do not know the Weighted Average Expected Return, you're investing almost without knowing what you are accomplishing (or trying to accomplish). The weighted average expected return should tell you very clearly what your portfolio is positioned to return to you periodically.

This is important because you could be earning a very low portfolio return, but taking much risk to do it. If half of your money is in growth mutual funds and half is in the bank, your portfolio might only return 8% annually, but you are taking on more risk then if you simply bought a U.S. government bond paying the same 8%, because the growth part of your portfolio could lose.

You calculate the weighted average expected return by determining the proportion of each investment to the total portfolio value. Then the expected returns on each investment are multiplied by their respective weight in the portfolio. The weighted average expected return for each investment is added together to reach the weighted average expected return for the portfolio:

For example, assume you own XYZ stock. The current market value is $6,000 with an expected return of 11%. Your other stock, ZZZ, has a current market value of $4,000 with an expected return of 14%.

HOW TO COMPUTE THE WEIGHTED AVERAGE EXPECTED RETURN:

Stock	Current Market Value	Expected Return	Percent of Portfolio
XYZ	6,000	11%	60%
ZZZ	4,000	4%	40%
Total Portfolio:	10,000		

.60 x 11 = .066
.40 x .14 = .056
.122, or 12.2%

12.2% IS THE AVERAGE EXPECTED RETURN

First you add the $6,000 and $4,000 to total $10,000. Then divide each number by the total ($6,000 divided by $10,000 and $4,000 divided by $10,000). The expected return for the $6,000 invested was 11%, so multiply the .60 by .11. Do the same for the $4,000 investment. Now, add the two and you have weighted average expected return. Move the decimals to put it back into a percentage and the product is the average expressed as a percentage.

Once you do this to your portfolio, I think a new realization will occur. You will see how investments such as money markets bring your average way down, yet highly speculative investments don't bring it way up. When considering what average return to use, try to get the average performance of the investment over the last ten years.

BETA COEFFICIENT AND PORTFOLIO RISK

A *Beta* is often referred to as the level of risk or volatility. Usually the benchmark used is the Standard and Poor's 500. The beta of the S&P 500 is "1." Now, if your investment has a beta greater then "1," your investment is probably more volatile (price swings are greater), than the market. This means your investment could be up considerably higher than the market, or considerably lower than the market. The rule of thumb is – the greater the beta, the more risk you take.

For instance, if your investment has a beta of "2" and the market was down 10%, your investment might be down 20%. However, if the market was up 10%, you could be up 20%. Ideally, if you have a growth portfolio, you would want to have a portfolio that had a beta of equal to or less than the market, with as good or better of a return than the market.

If all you wanted was steady income and minimal principal fluctuations, you might look for the highest yielding fund with a beta of .15. To find a beta of .15, you will probably find most of the funds will be high quality income funds and intermediate government and tax-free funds.

Whatever the objective of your portfolio, the beta will help you determine if your portfolio is being maximized. If your required rate of return is 8%, a good exercise would be to study all the mutual funds that have returned 8% over the last ten years and find the one with the lowest beta. After computing the beta for your entire portfolio, your beta should be on the low end, or you could be taking too much risk.

In other words, you might have a portfolio made up of all growth funds. Your average yield might be 10% with a beta of "1." However, if you could earn an 8% return by reallocating the portfolio, bring the beta down to .5, you have now maximized your portfolio by cutting your risk in half but only lowering your return by 2%. It makes sense if you don't really need to have a 10% return.

Your job is to calculate the portfolio beta coefficient. Basically taking all the betas of your different investments and determining the beta of your portfolio as a whole works like this.

Say you have two mutual funds called ABC and XYZ:

HOW TO CALCULATE THE BETA COEFFICIENT

	AMOUNT INVESTED	WEIGHT IN PORTFOLIO*	BETA	WEIGHTED BETA COEFFICIENT**
ABC Mutual Fund	$ 5,000	.25	1.2	.3
XYZ Mutual Fund	15,000	.75	.8	.6
TOTAL:	20,000			.9

* 5,000/20,000 = .25   ** .25 x 1.2 = .3
* 15,000/20,000 = .75   ** .75 x .8 = .6

THIS PORTFOLIO HAS AN AVERAGE BETA FACTOR OF .9

Finding the beta of any individual investment should be part of the criteria you include in your homework before investing. As discussed earlier, this information can easily be found by calling the company, asking your broker, going to the library and checking the *Value Line Reports* for stocks and *Lipper* or *Morningstar* for mutual funds.

In my opinion, a mature American will probably, on average, strive to achieve around an 8% to 10% true rate of return. Based on risk vs. reward the average portfolio beta, to earn 8% to 10%, should be no more then .6 to .7. In the financial planning section, we said it could be prudent to create your financial plan based on 90% of your true investable dollars. In the same way, don't consider the 10% of your assets that we don't include in the average. That 10% could be invested in pork bellies or a trip to Las Vegas – it doesn't matter so I don't figure in the return.

SAMPLE PORTFOLIO

Let's assume that in creating your financial plan and studying your situation, you have determined you need a 9% return and should do it with a beta of .6 or under.

Next, assume that over the last two years interest rates have been down, we have been in a recession, the global economy is having a tough time but the economy of the United States is looking brighter. Still, we have a new administration and that brings more uncertainty. The last time a Democrat was in office, inflation shot way up and interest rates with it. The stock and bond markets are reaching new highs and many people are saying the market is overvalued.

The only way to be successful is to remember one thing – the only constant is change. As long as you live, there will be pessimists, doomsayers and uncertainties. You must be prepared and invest wisely. Although there are numerous investments, they really break down to four categories: stocks, bonds, real estate and cash. All the other investments are usually just different ways to own these core holdings.

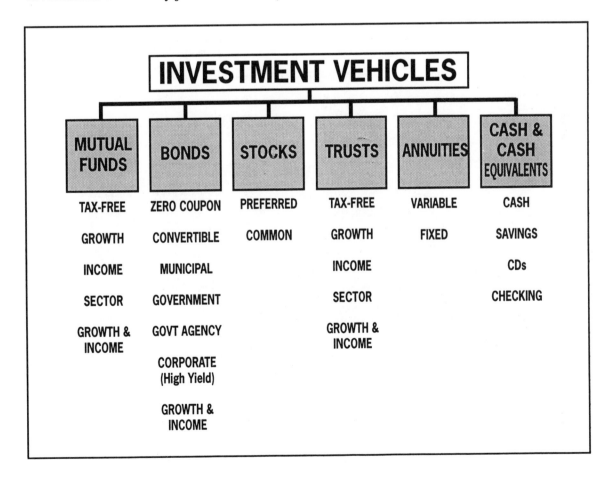

Now, let's also assume that you want moderate involvement in managing your portfolio and want to, on a limited basis, actively manage your accounts. By this I mean you will watch it, but want the freedom to take a three-month vacation. You would like a professional co-managing with you. Now that these parameters are established, we can decide how to best allocate your assets.

First, let's take care of the income. The financial plan already revealed that 9% return on your money is required. Let's assume that you only need 7% in income to live, with 2% going back into the estate for "extras" – nursing home costs, grandchildren's education fund, inflation, etc. Based on the economy and the understanding that interest rates might go up, this is a sample portfolio:

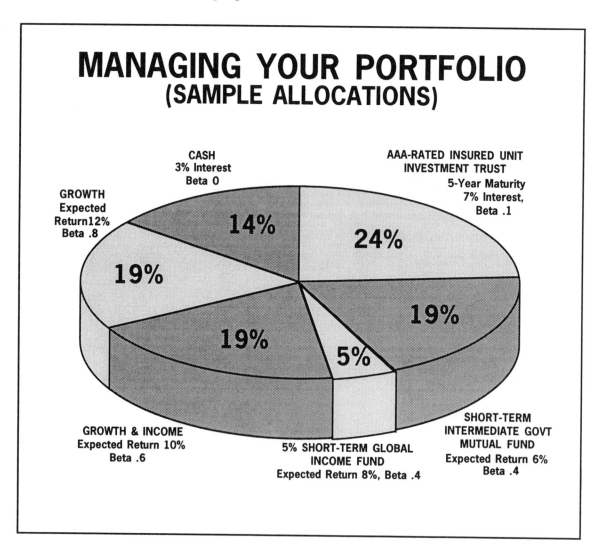

MANAGING YOUR PORTFOLIO
(SAMPLE ALLOCATIONS)

CASH
3% Interest
Beta 0

AAA-RATED INSURED UNIT
INVESTMENT TRUST
5-Year Maturity
7% Interest,
Beta .1

GROWTH
Expected
Return12%
Beta .8

14%

24%

19%

19%

19%

5%

GROWTH & INCOME
Expected Return 10%
Beta .6

5% SHORT-TERM GLOBAL
INCOME FUND
Expected Return 8%, Beta .4

SHORT-TERM
INTERMEDIATE GOVT
MUTUAL FUND
Expected Return 6%
Beta .4

THE FIRST 25%

Allocate 25% in a fixed AAA-rated, insured Unit Investment Trust (UIT) paying 7% to 8%. Although the price will fluctuate, it is more than enough income and you are guaranteed both interest and principal back upon maturity. You should not allocate more because this is a long-term maturity and chances are you will have to hold it the entire time. However, that doesn't matter, provided inflation doesn't get out of control, because you are receiving your required return.

Although you only need an average of 7% in income from the whole portfolio, let's take the full 8% (if you can get it) as income from this investment so we can allow one of the other investments to reinvest in an effort to grow.

If you want to diversify that 25% even further, you may want to allocate 15% in the UIT and 10% in a long-term government fund. By allocating some to a government mutual fund, you have a chance that the share price, over time, will rise, acting as an inflation hedge. I don't recommend more because when the belief is that interest rates may rise, the share price of that fund could go down.

You can also diversify this 25% in tax-free municipal bond funds if you feel that you need the tax free income.

THE NEXT 20%

Next, allocate 20% in a short-term/intermediate government-type mutual fund. This fund will probably will yield only 5% to 6% depending on interest rates at the time of purchase. The reason for the lower yield is because these are short-term obligations of the United States government. As interest rates rise, so should the interest rate on this fund and the principal should not fluctuate very much. This could be an ideal place for funds that you still want access to if you need to, but will give you a better return than a bank. Some call this the "CD alternative." So, leave only the bare essential in the bank and 20% in a fund.

THE NEXT 5%

Based on the economic situation discussed above, you might consider 5% in a high quality, short-term global income fund. This should give you an overall yield of between 7% and 9% (depending on current rates). The bonds of many foreign nations pay a higher interest rate. In addition, historically, foreign countries have followed our interest cycle. As rates stabilize and rise in the United States, they are usually starting to drop overseas. If you purchase a fund before it declines, you will still receive a nice interest rate and, when rates drop, an increase on your share price as well. The increase in share price will, again, act as your inflation hedge. Remember, when interest rates decline your share price increases.

A good case in point is the state of the economy during the years 1992 and 1993. U.S. government bond funds, on the average, performed extremely well between 1991 and 1992. As a result of interest rate declines, the share price of these funds increased. However, it was very difficult for the share price to continue rising on these funds unless rates dropped further. But how much further could they drop?

In the beginning of 1993, record numbers of dollars poured into these U.S. government funds. At the same time, disgruntled investors liquidated their investments in global government bond funds. Again, I ask why? Globally, interest rates were still high. The American rates were low. And statistics show foreign rates will usually decline following the United States. Yet more money went into the United States funds which had record low interest rates and investors were selling the global bond funds with higher rates. If rates decline globally your share price has a propensity to rise. If they remain status quo, then the rates overseas will probably be higher for longer time period than in the United States. This is the scientific aspect of investing. You might not know the timing, but you know it's the right thing to do technically. Timing is the artistic aspect of investing.

Investing in foreign countries may have more risk and you will need to be more careful in finding investments that will minimize your risk exposure. Seek investments that will only invest in government bonds of leading nations and only on a short-term basis. Make sure the manager has a good track record and is well respected. If things get touchy overseas, make sure you can pull out if you need to withdraw your funds.

ANOTHER 20%

Now, 20% of the portfolio should be positioned for both growth and income. When attempting to obtain both growth and income, it usually is not both the highest income and the highest growth, but the income is usually better than a CD rate and the growth is more conservative than a growth stock, which means it probably will not decline as dramatically as the market.

TWO IDEAS FOR INVESTORS TO OBTAIN BOTH GROWTH AND INCOME

1. ## INVEST IN ONE, TWO OR THREE GROWTH-AND-INCOME OR STRAIGHT-INCOME MUTUAL FUNDS.

   Take the income dividends generated by the fund and reinvest the capital gains. The income should average between 4% and 5%. Obviously many mutual funds brag about much higher percentages, but an investor should take a conservative approach.

   Because you took more income on previous investments, you can afford less income on this investment and you need the growth. Remember, if this part of your portfolio receives 5% growth, it is only on 15% of the portfolio. You will still need more growth to maintain purchasing power. When selecting these funds, try to keep the beta low, preferably under .6 and try to keep the alpha high. If you can find one that has never lost money, that would be another plus.

2. ## INVEST IN INDIVIDUAL STOCKS.

   Here's how to do this: Do your stock research and then pick five stocks you like. Make sure they all pay dividends of at least 5% to 6%. Be sure that the companies you select have a history of paying the dividend regularly. Try to find one that rarely or never cuts its dividend, but rather is always increasing it. Most dividends are paid quarterly, but many companies work off different quarters. So, make sure the dividends of the stocks you buy arrive in a different month in order to maintain your monthly income as opposed to getting a huge check every three months.

   Keep the beta of the portfolio at about .6. To receive that dividend your five stocks will probably consist of utility stocks, preferred stocks of major blue chip companies and possibly a convertible bond. A good rule of thumb is that if you cannot buy at least 100 shares per stock, the costs are too high and the diversification is not as great.

   Do your homework on how to pick a stock. Make sure that the companies you choose typically do well in the market. Look for stock growth that is in line with, or better than, inflation. Also, look at the stock performance in the years that the market was down. Find stocks that do not lose money when the market is down. Don't invest completely in utilities, as they are interest-sensitive and rates could rise. Pick a couple of high quality blue chips with very strong dividends. Now you will be getting the income of hopefully 6% along with growth, at least 4% per year, as a result of the price of your stock rising, giving you an overall return of 10%.

THE NEXT 15%

About 15% of a portfolio is usually growth. Obviously many kinds of growth potential exist and I encourage you to revert back to your financial plan to evaluate them. If all you need is the return from growth and income, with less risk, then perhaps you should increase the allocation on growth and income. However, if you need growth the best way is to go for the highest return with the lowest risk. If you are considering utilizing stocks or mutual funds, find the best returns with the lowest risk. Before actually looking for a specific mutual fund, determine your risk tolerance.

Say, for example, that you do not, under any circumstances, want a fund with a beta over .8 and an alpha under .45. If you research long-term growth funds, I can assure you that your list will be reduced to a only a handful that you can individually research.

One comment about growth that is often overlooked is that if you are successful at growth it will increase your taxes. If your income is increased and your taxes are increased, your Social Security may be taxed. Two prudent ways to avoid this possibility would be to place your growth assets in your IRA or a variable annuity for the tax deferral.

It always amazes me to look at a portfolio and see an investor's account comprised of stock in a liquid account and the IRA in bank CDs. That sounds backwards to me. Seriously reconsider keeping your IRAs in a bank or bank CD because the IRA is not taxed on the capital gain. If you are doing any mutual fund switching or timing, do it inside the IRA. The growth on your IRA is not figured into your gross income (which determines if you have to pay taxes on your Social Security) until you withdraw.

I'm sure your next question is, "Do we need the IRA for money because the income from our other investments is not enough?" My answer is another question – "Which is better, taking IRA money, paying the tax and then using it? Or using principal from your other investments?"

I would rather take principal from one of my other investments to live on than to disrupt my IRA. The reason is simple. When I use my principal, I am not taxed on it. So, even though I use it for income it is not considered on my income taxes which will lower my tax burden. It also will not increase my income if I am borderline on having to pay Social Security taxes.

If you plan your estate correctly by the time you have to take the IRA, your income should be in the lowest bracket, and, because that money compounded for so long at a tax-deferred rate, even if taxes are high the difference on the tax-deferred compounding is significant.

As noted in the variable annuity discussion, many annuities will allow you to invest in the most popular mutual funds while you never have to lose control of your money or begin withdrawing as with an IRA. Many have no front-end commissions, although some have a penalty for early withdrawal. However, this vehicle allows you to realize no taxable gain until withdrawal.

Many people are successful with the growth portion of their portfolio, and as a result they incur capital gains. But in an IRA or annuity you can sell a mutual fund, place the proceeds in a money market all inside the annuity, and avoid all the capital gains. Then your income would be reduced, lowering your taxes and protecting you from Social Security taxes.

Finally, don't forget that you can find growth investment in places other than American stocks. It is always interesting when someone asks me what I think of the market. I always ask, "Which one?" There is the domestic stock market, bond market, overseas equities, overseas debt, real estate market and more. Usually markets work very much like the principles of physics. When there is an action, there is a reaction. If one market goes up, another goes down. If interest rates begin to rise domestically, they may still be declining overseas. If the United States is experiencing a recession, it is likely another country is in an expansion/growth phase which you could probably find a mutual fund of that country. Or, just staying on United States soil, if we start to experience high inflation, bonds probably will perform poorly, but real estate usually does very well in inflationary times. Although not fashionable right now, real estate has been depressed, stocks have been doing terrific, pretty soon the tables will be turned. The bottom line being...***don't have tunnel vision***...look at the future, not at the past, and broaden your horizons when considering growth.

THE FINAL 15%

Leave the final 15% in cash. Although some investors may feel that is an excessive amount, you will need liquid cash to make the plan successful. The reason is because of the averaging effect. I repeat, everything is cyclical. You might average more into a mutual fund or a stock if your plan calls for it and find the next day that negative economic news comes out forcing your investment lower. However, the investment may have been dragged down with the rest of the market but may still be a viable investment. The way to truly take advantage of this is by systematically averaging more, especially after a sell-off like the one just described. By all means don't frivolously sell your investment but have cash ready to average more. This strategy is known as dollar-cost averaging and is one of the best ways to reduce risk and increase portfolio return. Then, when one investment is "overbought" and it's time to sell, you can replenish your cash.

HOW TO MONITOR THE PLAN

Obviously the investment plan has to be continually monitored. However, often times when people monitor their plan they make changes. ***Don't make changes unless it is absolutely necessary.*** Or, make changes but the right ones. Common mistakes might be on your long-term growth accounts that might start averaging down for a long period of time (one year or more). The account should not be sold, and you should use the reserves to average more. Or, average the profits from another account if that account is now overvalued. If you did your homework and know the fund is good and this is simply a correction, then take advantage of the opportunity of buying some shares on sale.

Also, look at your profits. If you have made the return you wanted, don't be afraid to sell. It's often said that the easy part is buying, the hard part is selling. Simply revert back to your plan. If you expected your growth account to make 20% and it did it in two months, perhaps you should take a profit and wait for it to correct a bit (if you feel it is overvalued).

Another excellent example is what happened with bond funds in the early '90s. The funds not only paid the dividend expected, but for the most part, had an excellent appreciation of the shares. The reason was the lower interest rates. You must say to yourself, "This is an economic cycle. How much further can interest rates drop? Is the probability greater that they will rise or drop even lower?"

If you think rates might rise and you have a handsome profit, again consider selling, taking the profit and finding an alternative investment in the same asset class. Consider the percentage (rate of return) you will make from selling (after paying the tax). Even if you had to place the funds in a short-term government account for up to a year earning a dividend of 1% less than what your other investment was earning, will making the switch and capturing the profit still be worth it?

Speaking of economic cycles, watch the markets. If domestic interest rates have continually been dropping, some people think that the foreign rates will follow the trend. Without seriously increasing your risk you might want to average into that type of investment to take advantage of the declining interest rates such as we experienced with domestic rates.

When monitoring your portfolio you must be a forward thinker and be patient. Economic cycles could last three, five or even more years. How will your plan be affected if interest rates rise? How will your plan be affected if inflation takes off? What usually happens over the first few years when a Democrat takes office? Is your portfolio properly diversified to take advantage of it? So, if you look at the next four years you might say, "Okay, a Democrat is in office, taxes have a propensity to rise, as well as inflation. More environmental programs will begin and with all this might come higher interest rates. We are in a fairly strong, but nervous recovery period."

In the circumstances outlined above, what should you do? Perhaps you should allocate a portion of the portfolio that should do well if interest rates rise, but not suffer if they don't. Find some tax-advantaged investments and perhaps look at stocks, bonds or funds that might do well under a Democratic leadership such as those which help build our infrastructure, or support environmentally-friendly companies. Also, take profits on investments that did well in declining interest rate cycles and look globally to see if any value is out that way.

Remember, your retirement should be a long and happy one. Once you set the plan for the long haul, you can fine tune it as market conditions change, but the overall allocation should be kept almost the same unless your needs change. Try hard not to stray from your plan or make any unnecessary changes. Think like a technician and try to avoid emotional decisions.

DOLLAR-COST AVERAGING

Since we have discussed it so much a further definition is warranted.

Dollar-cost averaging is a systematic savings plan that will help you reduce the price you pay for investments, reduce risk and hopefully increase return. The old saying of "buy low and sell high" is not that easy to do. However, if you can make a commitment to add to your stock the same amount of money, at the same time every month (or quarter), you will take advantage of all the highs and the lows and reduce your average cost per share. In rising market environments you will be purchasing fewer shares and during declining markets, more shares.

For instance, assume you invest $1,000 per month for nine consecutive months at different market prices. Over nine months you invested $9,000 but let's take a hypothetical example to see if your money is still worth $9,000.

$1,000 PER MONTH INVESTMENT

Months	Share Price	No. of Shares Purchased w/$1,000	Cumulative Market Value
1	$ 8	125	$ 1,000
2	10	100	2,250
3	8	125	2,800
4	5	200	2,750
5	4	250	3,200
6	5	200	5,000
7	8	125	9,000
8	10	100	12,250
9	8	125	10,800

The hypothetical example above shows your portfolio has grown to more than $10,800. You invested a total of $9,000.

Note: **Cumulative Market Value** *is found by adding the number of shares owned in total for that period and multiplying it by the share price for that period. So, in period three, you already owned a total of 350 shares, the current share price was 8 giving you a dollar value of $2,800.*

CONCLUSION

We have discussed and outlined many issues pertaining to financial investments, estate planning and health care. Focus on just one aspect at a time in order to get your plan in place, and your life so much more pleasant. Do not become confused the complexities of each topic or attempt to become an expert in any of them or you will become a *jack of all trades and an master at none.* Ultimately, you will accomplish little more than personal frustration.

You can be confident that you know the most important guidelines if you just remember the three main objectives you are striving to accomplish with your estate and financial plan. They are:

CONTROL, PRESERVATION and MAXIMIZATION

If your assets are held in joint tenancy, determine if that is the best way for you to hold title, and if are you maintaining ***control*** of your estate. If not, refer to the sections covering Estate Planning.

If you are paying unnecessary taxes, you are not ***preserving*** your estate. Re-examine the sections on Taxes and determine if you are really conserving your dollars.

If you are taking too much risk for your return on investments, you are not ***maximizing*** your finances. Refer to the sections covering Investments and Asset Allocations.

If you take these steps one at a time, it will become very easy to accomplish your goals.

Your best years are ahead of you. Therefore, enjoy them by building memories, reflecting on your accomplishments, beginning new interests and traveling as much as possible. If you manage your finances and investments prudently, the fruits of your endeavors will be much sweeter during your retirement.

APPENDIX

DIRECTORY OF STATE INSURANCE DEPARTMENTS
AND AGENCIES ON AGING

Each state has its own laws and regulations governing all types of insurance. The insurance offices listed in the left column of this directory are responsible for enforcing the laws, as well as providing the public with information about insurance. The agencies on aging, listed in the right column, are responsible for coordinating services for older Americans. The middle column lists the telephone number to call for insurance counseling services. Calls to an 800 number are free when made within the respective state.

INSURANCE DEPARTMENTS	INSURANCE COUNSELING	AGENCIES ON AGING
Insurance Department 135 South Union Street Montgomery, AL 36130-3401 (205) 269-3550	Alabama 1-800-242-5463	Commission on Aging 770 Washington Ave., Suite 470 Montgomery, AL 36130 (800) 243-5463, (205) 242-5743
Division of Insurance 800 E. Diamond, Suite 560 Anchorage, AK 99515 (907) 349-1230	Alaska (907) 563-5654	Older Alaskans Commission P.O. Box C MS 0209 Juneau, AK 99811 (907) 465-3250
Insurance Department Office of the Governor Ago, AS 96797 011-684/633-4116	American Samoa	Territorial Administration on Aging Government of American Samoa Ago Pago, AS 96799 (684) 633-1251
Insurance Department Consumer Affairs/Investigation Div. 3030 N. Third Street Phoenix, AZ 85012 (602) 255-4783	Arizona (800) 432-4040	Dept. of Economic Security Aging & Adult Administration 1789 W. Jefferson Street Phoenix, AZ 85007 (602) 542-4446
Insurance Department Seniors Insurance Network 1123 S. University 400 University Tower Building Little Rock, AR 72204 (501) 686-2900	Arkansas (800) 852-5494	Division of Aging & Adult Services Donaghey Plaza South Seventh & Main Streets, Suite 1417 P.O. Box 1417, Slot 1412 Little Rock, AR 72203-1437 (501) 682-2441
Insurance Department Consumer Services Division 3450 Wilshire Blvd. Los Angeles, CA 90010 (800) 927-4357	California (800) 927-4357	Department of Aging 1600 K Street Sacramento, CA 95814 (916) 322-3887
Insurance Division 1560 Broadway, Suite 850 Denver, CO 80202 (303) 894-7499	Colorado (303) 894-7499	Aging and Adult Services Department of Social Services 1575 Sherman Street, Tenth Floor Denver, CO 80203-1714 (303) 866-3851

INSURANCE DEPARTMENTS	INSURANCE COUNSELING	AGENCIES ON AGING
	Commonwealth of the Northern Mariana Islands	Dept. of Community & Cultural Affairs Civic Center Commonwealth of the Northern Mariana Islands Saipan, CM 96950 (607) 234-6011
Insurance Department 153 Market Street P.O. Box 816 Hartford, CT 06142-0816 (203) 297-3800	Connecticut (800) 443-9946	Department on Aging 175 Main Street Hartford, CT 06106 1-800-443-9946 (203) 566-7772
Insurance Department 841 Silver Lake Blvd. Dover, DE 19901 (302) 739-4251	Delaware (800) 851-3535	Division of Aging Dept.. of Health & Social Services 11901 DuPont Highway New Castle, DE 19720 (302) 577-4660
Insurance Department 613 G Street, NW, Room 638 P.O. Box 37200 Washington, D.C. 20001-7200 (202) 727-8009	District of Columbia (202) 724-5626	Office on Aging 1424 K Street, NW, Second Floor Washington, D.C. 20005 (202) 724-5626 (202) 724-5622
	Federated States of Micronesia	State Agency on Aging Office of Health Services Federated States of Micronesia Ponape, E.C.I. 96941
Department of Insurance State Capitol, Plaza 11 Tallahassee, FL 32399-0300 (800) 342-2762 (904) 922-3100	Florida (904) 922-2073	Office on Aging & Adult Services 1317 Winewood Blvd. Building 2, Room 323 Tallahassee, FL 32399-0700 (904) 488-8922
Insurance Department 2 Martin L. King, Jr. Drive Room 716., West Tower Atlanta, GA 30334 (404) 656-2056	Georgia (404) 894-5333	Office of Aging Department of Human Resources 878 Peachtree St., NE, Room 632 Atlanta, GA 30309 (404) 894-5333
Insurance Department 855 W. Marine Drive P.O. Box 2796 Agana, Guam 96910 011 (671) 477-5144	Guam	Division of Senior Citizens Dept. of Public Health/Social Services P.O. Box 2816 Agana, Guam 96910 011 (671) 734-4361
Dept. of Commerce/Consumer Affairs Insurance Division P.O. Box 3614 Honolulu, HI 96811 (808) 586-2790	Hawaii (808) 586-0100	Executive Office on Aging 335 Merchant Street Room 241 Honolulu, HI 96813 (808) 586-0100

INSURANCE DEPARTMENTS	INSURANCE COUNSELING	AGENCIES ON AGING
Insurance Department Public Service Department 500 S. Tenth Street Boise, ID 83720 (208) 334-4350	Idaho (800) 247-4422	Office on Aging Statehouse, Room 108 Boise, ID 83720 (208) 334-3833
Insurance Department 320 W. Washington St., 4th Floor Springfield, IL 62767 (217) 782-4515	Illinois (800) 548-9034	Department on Aging 421 E. Capitol Avenue Springfield, IL 62701 (217) 785-2870
Insurance Department 311 W. Washington St., Suite 300 Indianapolis, IN 46204 1-800-622-4461 (317) 232-2395	Indiana (800) 452-4800	Department of Human Services 402 W. Washington Street P.O. Box 7083 Indianapolis, IN 46207-7083 (317) 232-7020
Insurance Division Lucas State Office Building E. 12th & Grand Streets, 6th Floor Des Moines, IA 50319 (515) 281-5705	Iowa (515) 281-5705	Department of Elder Affairs Jewett Building, Suite 236 914 Grand Avenue Des Moines, IA 50309 (515) 281-5187
Insurance Department 420 S.W. Ninth Street Topeka, KS 66612 (913) 296-3071 (800) 432-2484	Kansas (800) 432-3535	Department of Aging 122-S. Docking State Office Building 915 S.W. Harrison Topeka, KS 66612-1500 (913) 296-4986
Insurance Department 229 W. Main Street P.O. Box 517 Frankfort, KY 40602 (502) 564-3630	Kentucky (800) 372-2973	Division of Aging Services Department of Social Services 275 E. Main Street Frankfort, KY 40621 (502) 564-6930
Insurance Department P.O. Box 94214 Baton Rouge, LA 70804-9214 (504) 342-5900 (800) 259-5301	Louisiana (800) 259-5301	Governor's Office of Elderly Affairs 4550 N. Boulevard P.O. Box 80374 Baton Rouge, LA 70896-0374 (504) 925-1700
Bureau of Insurance Consumer Division State House, Station 34 August, ME 04333 (207) 582-8707	Maine (800) 750-5353	Bureau of Elder & Adult Services 35 Anthony Avenue, Station 11 August, ME 04333 (207) 624-5335
Insurance Department Complaints & Investigation Unit 501 St. Paul Place Baltimore, MD 21202-2272 (410) 333-6300	Maryland (800) 243-3425	State Agency on Aging 301 W. Preston Street Room 1004 Baltimore, MD 21201 (410) 225-1102

INSURANCE DEPARTMENTS	INSURANCE COUNSELING	AGENCIES ON AGING
Insurance Division Consumer Services Section 280 Friend Street Boston, MA 02114 (617) 727-7189	Massachusetts (617) 727-7750	Executive Office of Elder Affairs 1 Ashburton Place, Fifth Floor Boston, MA 02108 1-800-882-2003 (617) 727-7750
Insurance Department P.O. Box 30220 Lansing, MI 48909 (517) 373-0220	Michigan (517) 373-8230	Office of Services to the Aging 611 W. Ottawa Street P.O. Box 30026 Lansing, MI 48909 (517) 373-8230
Insurance Department Department of Commerce 133 E. Seventh Street St. Paul, MN 55101-2362 (612) 296-4026	Minnesota (800) 392-0343	Board on Aging Human Services Building 444 Lafayette Road St. Paul, MN 55155-3843 (612) 296-2770
Insurance Department Consumer Assistance Division P.O. Box 79 Jackson, MS 39205 (601) 359-3569	Mississippi (Counseling services are not provided at this time.)	Council on Aging 455 N. Lamar Street Jackson, MS 39202 1-800-345-6347 (601) 359-6770
Department of Insurance Consumer Services Section P.O. Box 690 Jefferson City, MO 65102-0690 (800) 726-7390 (314) 751-2640	Missouri (800) 726-7390	Division on Aging Department of Social Services P.O. Box 1337 615 Howerton Court Jefferson City, MO 65102-1337 (314) 751-3082
Insurance Department 126 N. Sanders, Mitchell Bldg., Rm 270 P.O. Box 4009 Helena, MT 59604 (800) 332-6148, (406) 444-2040	Montana 1-800-332-2272	The Governor's Office on Aging State Capital Building, Room 219 Helena, MT 59620 (800) 332-2272 (406) 444-3111
Insurance Department Terminal Building 941 O Street, Suite 400 Lincoln, NE 68508 (402) 471-2201	Nebraska (402) 471-4887	Department on Aging State Office Building 301 Centennial Mall South Lincoln, NE 68509-5044 (402) 471-2306
Department of Insurance Consumer Services 1665 Hot Springs Road Capitol Complex Carson City, NV 89701 (702) 687-4270, (800) 992-0900	Nevada (702) 687-4270	Department of Human Resources Division of Aging Services 340 N. 11th Street, Suite 114 Las Vegas, NV 89101 (702) 486-3545
Insurance Department Life and Health Division 169 Manchester Street Concord, NH 03301 (603) 271-2261, (800) 852-3416	New Hampshire (603) 271-4642	Dept. of Health & Human Services Division of Elderly & Adult Services 6 Hazen Drive Concord, NH 03301 (603) 271-4680

INSURANCE DEPARTMENTS	INSURANCE COUNSELING	AGENCIES ON AGING
Insurance Department 20 W. State Street Roebling Building Trenton, NJ 08625 (609) 292-5360	New Jersey (800) 792-8820	Department of Community Affairs Division on Aging S. Broad & Front Streets, CN 807 Trenton, NJ 08625-0807 (800) 792-8820, (609) 292 0920
Insurance Department P.O. Box 1269 Santa Fe, NM 87504-1269 (505) 827-4500	New Mexico (800) 432-2080	Agency on Aging La Villa Rivera Building, First Floor 224 E. Palace Avenue Santa Fe, NM 87501 (800) 432-2080, (505) 827-7640
Insurance Department 160 W. Broadway New York, NY 10013 (212) 602-0203 Outside of New York City (800) 342-3736	New York (800) 342-9871	State Office for the Aging 2 Empire State Plaza Albany, NY 12223-0001 (800) 342-9871 (518) 474-5731
Insurance Department Seniors Health Insurance Information Program (SHIIP) P.O. Box 26387 Raleigh, NC 27611 (919) 733-0111 (SHIIP) (800) 662-7777 (Customer Services)	North Carolina (800) 443-9354	Department of Human Resources Division of Aging 693 Palmer Drive Raleigh, NC 27626-0531 (919) 733-3983
Insurance Department Capitol Building, Fifth Floor 600 E. Boulevard Bismarck, ND 58505-0320 (800) 247-0560, (701) 224-2440	North Dakota (800) 247-0560	Department of Human Services Aging Services Division State Capitol Building Bismarck, ND 58507-7070 (701) 224-2577
Insurance Department Consumer Services Division 2100 Stella Court Columbus, OH 43266-0566 (800) 686-1526, (614) 644-2673	Ohio (800) 686-1578	Department of Aging 50 W. Broad Street, Eighth Floor Columbus, OH 43266-0501 (614) 466-1221
Insurance Department P.O. Box 53408 Oklahoma City. OK 73152-3408 (405) 521-2828	Oklahoma (405) 521-6628	Department of Human Services Aging Services Division 312 NE 28th Street Oklahoma City, OK 73125 (405) 521-2327
Department of Insurance & Finance Insurance Div. Consumer Advocacy 440 Labor & Industries Building Salem, OR 97310 (503) 378-4484	Oregon (503) 378-4484	Dept. of Human Resources Senior Services Division 500 Summer St. NE, 2nd Floor Salem, OR 97310 (800) 232-3020, (503) 378-4728
	Palau	State Agency on Aging Department of Social Services Republic of Palau Koror, Palau 96940

INSURANCE DEPARTMENTS	INSURANCE COUNSELING	AGENCIES ON AGING
Insurance Department Consumer Services Bureau 1321 Strawberry Square Harrisburg, PA 17120 (717) 787-2317	Pennsylvania (717) 783-8975	Department of Aging 231 State Street Barto Building Harrisburg, PA 17101 (717) 783-1550
Insurance Department Fernandez Juncos Station P.O. Box 8330 Santurce, PR 00910 (809) 722-8686	Puerto Rico (809) 721-5710	Governors Office of Elderly Affairs Gericulture Commission Box 11398 Santurce, PR 00910 (809) 722-2429
	Republic of the Marshall Islands	State Agency on Aging Department of Social Services Republic of the Marshall Islands Marjuro, Marshall Islands 96960
Insurance Division 233 Richmond St., Suite 233 Providence, RI 02903-4233 (401) 277-2223	Rhode Island (800) 322-2880	Department of Elderly Affairs 160 Pine Street Providence, RI 02903 (401) 277-2858
Insurance Department Consumer Assistance Section P.O. Box 100105 Columbia, SC 29202-3105 (803) 737-6140, (800) 768-3467	South Carolina (800) 868-9095	Commission on Aging 400 Arbor Lake Drive Suite B-500 Columbia, SC 29223 (803) 735-0210
Insurance Department Enforcement 910 E. Sioux Avenue Pierre, SD 57501-3940 (605) 773-3563	South Dakota (605) 773-3656	Agency on Aging Richard F. Kneip Building 700 Governors Drive Pierre, SD 57501-2291 (605) 773-3656
Department of Commerce & Insurance Insurance Assistance Office, 4th Floor 400 James, Robertson Parkway Nashville, TN 37243 (800) 525-2816, (615) 741-4955	Tennessee 1-800-525-2816	Commission on Aging 706 Church Street Suite 201 Nashville, TN 37243-0860 (615) 741-2056
Department of Insurance Complaints Resolution, MC 111-1A 333 Guadalupe St., P.O. Box 149091 Austin , TX 78714-9091 (512) 463-6515 (800) 252-3439	Texas (800) 252-9240	Department on Aging P.O. Box 12786 Capitol Station 949 U.S. Route 35 South Austin, TX 78741 (512) 444-2727
Insurance Department Consumer Services 3110 State Office Building Salt Lake City, UT 84114 (800) 439-3805, (801) 538-3805	Utah (801) 538-3910	Division of Aging & Adult Services 120 North 200 West P.O. Box 45500 Salt Lake City, UT 84103 (801) 538-3910

INSURANCE DEPARTMENTS	INSURANCE COUNSELING	AGENCIES ON AGING
Department of Banking & Insurance Consumer Complaint Division 89 Main Street, Drawer 20 Montpelier, VT 05602-3101 (802) 828-3301	Vermont (800) 642-5119	Office on Aging Waterbury Complex 103 S. Main Street Waterbury, VT 05671-2301 (802) 241-2400
Insurance Department Kongens Garde No. 18 St. Thomas, VI 00802 (809) 774-2991	Virgin Islands (809) 774-2991	Department of Human Services 19 Estate Diamond, Fredrick Sted St. Croix, VI 00840 (809) 772-4850
Insurance Department Consumer Services Division 700 Jefferson Building P.O. Box 1157 Richmond, VA 23209 (804) 786-7691	Virginia (800) 552-4464	Department for the Aging 700 Centre, Tenth Floor 700 E. Franklin Street Richmond, VA 23219-2327 (800) 552-4464 (804) 225-2271
Insurance Department Insurance Building AQ21 P.O. Box 40255 Olympia, WA 98504-0255 (800) 562-6900 (206) 753-7300	Washington (800) 562-6900	Aging/Adult Services Administration Dept. of Social & Health Services 12th & Jefferson Streets Mail Stop OB-44-A Olympia, WA 98504 (206) 586-3768
Insurance Department 2019 Washington Street E. Charleston, WV 25305 (304) 348-3386 (800) 642-9004 (800) 435-7381 (Hearing Impaired)	West Virginia (304) 558-3317	Commission on Aging State Capitol Complex Holly Grove Charleston, WV 25305 (304) 558-3317
Insurance Department Complaints Department P.O. Box 7873 Madison, WI 53707 (800) 236-8517 (608) 266-0103	Wisconsin (800) 242-1060	Bureau on Aging Dept. of Health & Social Services P.O. Box 7851 217 S. Hamilton St., Suite 300 Madison, WI 53707 (608) 266-2536
Insurance Department Herschler Building 122 W. 25th Street Cheyenne, WY 82002 (800) 442-4333 (307) 777-7401	Wyoming (800) 442-4333 Ext. 6888	Division on Aging Hathaway Building 2300 Capitol Avenue, Room 139 Cheyenne, WY 82002 (800) 442-2766 (307) 777-7986

COMPOUNDING INTEREST CHART

TABLE I

Compound Growth Rate (Investment Rate of Return and Inflation Factors)

Years	4.0%	4.5%	5.0%	5.5%	6.0%	6.5%	7.0%	7.5%	8.0%	8.5%	9.0%	9.5%	10.0%	10.5%	11.0%	11.5%	12.0%	Years
1	1.04	1.05	1.05	1.06	1.06	1.07	1.07	1.08	1.08	1.09	1.09	1.10	1.10	1.11	1.11	1.12	1.12	1
2	1.08	1.09	1.10	1.11	1.12	1.13	1.14	1.16	1.17	1.18	1.19	1.20	1.21	1.22	1.23	1.24	1.25	2
3	1.12	1.14	1.16	1.17	1.19	1.21	1.23	1.24	1.26	1.28	1.30	1.31	1.33	1.35	1.37	1.39	1.40	3
4	1.17	1.19	1.22	1.24	1.26	1.29	1.31	1.34	1.36	1.39	1.41	1.44	1.46	1.49	1.52	1.55	1.57	4
5	1.22	1.25	1.28	1.31	1.34	1.37	1.40	1.44	1.47	1.50	1.54	1.57	1.61	1.65	1.69	1.72	1.76	5
6	1.27	1.30	1.34	1.38	1.42	1.46	1.50	1.54	1.59	1.63	1.68	1.72	1.77	1.82	1.87	1.92	1.97	6
7	1.32	1.36	1.41	1.45	1.50	1.55	1.61	1.66	1.71	1.77	1.83	1.89	1.95	2.01	2.08	2.14	2.21	7
8	1.37	1.42	1.48	1.53	1.59	1.65	1.72	1.78	1.85	1.92	1.99	2.07	2.14	2.22	2.30	2.39	2.48	8
9	1.42	1.49	1.55	1.62	1.69	1.76	1.84	1.92	2.00	2.08	2.17	2.26	2.36	2.46	2.56	2.66	2.77	9
10	1.48	1.55	1.63	1.71	1.79	1.88	1.97	2.06	2.16	2.26	2.37	2.48	2.59	2.71	2.84	2.97	3.11	10
11	1.54	1.62	1.71	1.80	1.90	2.00	2.10	2.22	2.33	2.45	2.58	2.71	2.85	3.00	3.15	3.31	3.48	11
12	1.60	1.70	1.80	1.90	2.01	2.13	2.25	2.38	2.52	2.66	2.81	2.97	3.14	3.31	3.50	3.69	3.90	12
13	1.67	1.77	1.89	2.01	2.13	2.27	2.41	2.56	2.72	2.89	3.07	3.25	3.45	3.66	3.88	4.12	4.36	13
14	1.73	1.85	1.98	2.12	2.26	2.41	2.58	2.75	2.94	3.13	3.34	3.56	3.80	4.05	4.31	4.59	4.89	14
15	1.80	1.94	2.08	2.23	2.40	2.57	2.76	2.96	3.17	3.40	3.64	3.90	4.18	4.47	4.78	5.12	5.47	15
16	1.87	2.02	2.18	2.36	2.54	2.74	2.95	3.18	3.43	3.69	3.97	4.27	4.59	4.94	5.31	5.71	6.13	16
17	1.95	2.11	2.29	2.48	2.69	2.92	3.16	3.42	3.70	4.00	4.33	4.68	5.05	5.46	5.90	6.36	6.87	17
18	2.03	2.21	2.41	2.62	2.85	3.11	3.38	3.68	4.00	4.34	4.72	5.12	5.56	6.03	6.54	7.09	7.69	18
19	2.11	2.31	2.53	2.77	3.03	3.31	3.62	3.95	4.32	4.71	5.14	5.61	6.12	6.67	7.26	7.91	8.61	19
20	2.19	2.41	2.65	2.92	3.21	3.52	3.87	4.25	4.66	5.11	5.60	6.14	6.73	7.37	8.06	8.82	9.65	20
21	2.28	2.52	2.79	3.08	3.40	3.75	4.14	4.57	5.03	5.55	6.11	6.73	7.40	8.14	8.95	9.83	10.80	21
22	2.37	2.63	2.93	3.25	3.60	4.00	4.43	4.91	5.44	6.02	6.66	7.36	8.14	8.99	9.93	10.97	12.10	22
23	2.46	2.75	3.07	3.43	3.82	4.26	4.74	5.28	5.87	6.53	7.26	8.06	8.95	9.94	11.03	12.23	13.55	23
24	2.56	2.88	3.23	3.61	4.05	4.53	5.07	5.67	6.34	7.08	7.91	8.83	9.85	10.98	12.24	13.63	15.18	24
25	2.67	3.01	3.39	3.81	4.29	4.83	5.43	6.10	6.85	7.69	8.62	9.67	10.83	12.14	13.59	15.20	17.00	25
26	2.77	3.14	3.56	4.02	4.55	5.14	5.81	6.56	7.40	8.34	9.40	10.59	11.92	13.41	15.08	16.95	19.04	26
27	2.88	3.28	3.73	4.24	4.82	5.48	6.21	7.05	7.99	9.05	10.25	11.59	13.11	14.82	16.74	18.90	21.32	27
28	3.00	3.43	3.92	4.48	5.11	5.83	6.65	7.58	8.63	9.82	11.17	12.69	14.42	16.37	18.58	21.07	23.88	28
29	3.12	3.58	4.12	4.72	5.42	6.21	7.11	8.14	9.32	10.65	12.17	13.90	15.86	18.09	20.62	23.49	26.75	29
30	3.24	3.75	4.32	4.98	5.74	6.61	7.61	8.75	10.06	11.56	13.27	15.22	17.45	19.99	22.89	26.20	29.96	30
31	3.37	3.91	4.54	5.26	6.09	7.04	8.15	9.41	10.87	12.54	14.46	16.67	19.19	22.09	25.41	29.21	33.56	31
32	3.51	4.09	4.76	5.55	6.45	7.50	8.72	10.12	11.74	13.61	15.76	18.25	21.11	24.41	28.21	32.57	37.58	32
33	3.65	4.27	5.00	5.85	6.84	7.99	9.33	10.88	12.68	14.76	17.18	19.98	23.23	26.97	31.31	36.31	42.09	33
34	3.79	4.47	5.25	6.17	7.25	8.51	9.98	11.69	13.69	16.02	18.73	21.88	25.55	29.81	34.75	40.49	47.14	34
35	3.95	4.67	5.52	6.51	7.69	9.06	10.68	12.57	14.79	17.38	20.41	23.96	28.10	32.94	38.57	45.15	52.80	35

A-8

GLOSSARY OF TERMS